· A HISTORY LOVER'S ·
GUIDE TO

MOBILE AND THE
ALABAMA GULF COAST

· A HISTORY LOVER'S ·
GUIDE TO
MOBILE AND THE
ALABAMA GULF COAST

JOE CUHAJ

THE
History
PRESS

Published by The History Press
Charleston, SC
www.historypress.com

Frontispiece: The founder of the city, Jean Baptiste Le Moyne, Sieur de Bienville, proudly stands before modern-day Mobile along the city's waterfront at Cooper's Riverside Park. *Author's collection.*

First published 2023

Manufactured in the United States

ISBN 9781467152709

Library of Congress Control Number: 2022948302

Notice: The information in this book is true and complete to the best of our knowledge. It is offered without guarantee on the part of the author or The History Press. The author and The History Press disclaim all liability in connection with the use of this book.

This book is dedicated to those who seek the truth in history.

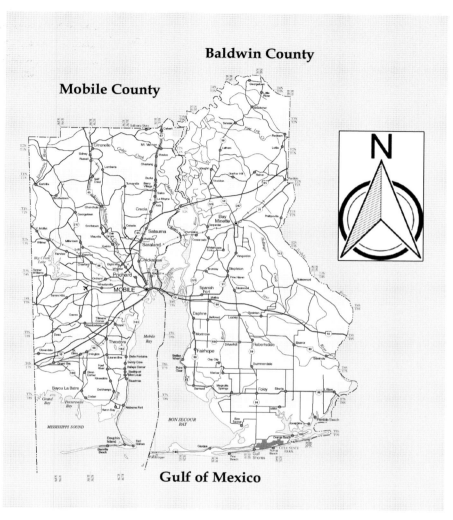

An overview map of Mobile and Baldwin Counties on the Alabama Gulf Coast.
Author's collection.

CONTENTS

PREFACE

Several rivers flow southward, bringing runoff from a substantial portion of the southeastern United States toward the Gulf of Mexico, spreading out across 260,000 acres of land to form an intricate network of bayous and channels, the second-largest river delta in the country, the Mobile-Tensaw River Delta.

When the flooding rains come, these channels spill out from their banks to spread their nutrient-rich waters across the land, creating a unique fertile environment reminiscent of the Amazon where an amazing variety of plant and animal life flourish before these tributaries and rivers converge to create the wide Mobile Bay, which eventually flows into the Gulf of Mexico.

It is here, along the banks of that delta, bay and the gleaming white shores of the Gulf that Alabama's oldest city, and one of the oldest along the northern Gulf Coast of the United States, was founded more than 320 years ago: Mobile.

When I moved to the Mobile area more than forty years ago, my knowledge of the Alabama Gulf Coast was limited save for the history of the Battle of Mobile Bay, which I learned of during my navy boot camp training and Hurricane Frederick, which devastated the area in 1979. My wife (who is from Mobile) and I were both in the U.S. Navy and were dating at the time in Norfolk, Virginia. We followed the storm's progress intently because her family still lived in Mobile.

I have always loved history. Why I didn't pursue it as a career path is beyond me. My career choice took a different path, and I became an armchair

This ancient resident of the Mobile–Tensaw River Delta keeps a watchful eye out. *Author's collection.*

historian. Once we moved to Mobile, I learned of the city's incredible and intricate history and immediately fell in love with the Port City. Or is it the Azalea City, so named for the azaleas that flame red, white and pink along many of the streets in spring? Or is it the Mother of Mystics, a name the city garnered from the fact that it was the birthplace of Mardi Gras in the United States? Doesn't matter. Choose your moniker, but no matter what you call it, the history of Mobile is truly fascinating.

I have been quite fortunate to have had the opportunity to write a little bit about the city's history since moving to Mobile in 1981 in my many outdoor recreation books where I take hikers and kayakers to some of the interesting historical landmarks found not only in Mobile but also across Alabama—landmarks that cannot be found in a museum. They can only be reached by foot or paddle. I was also fortunate to have been asked to write two historical nonfiction books dealing directly with Mobile history. The first was *Baseball in Mobile* (Arcadia Publishing, 2004). Along with my coauthor, Tamra Carraway, the book presented a very cursory look at the sport's history in Mobile, which, as we found, was so deep, dating back to the mid-1800s, that it was too much to include all of it in that small book.

That history includes the fact that the city was the birthplace of five Hall of Fame players—Satchel Paige, Henry "Hank" Aaron, Willie McCovey, Ozzie Smith and Billy Williams—making it third behind New York and Los Angeles for producing the most Hall of Famers. We also discovered that Mobile played a role in making baseball the national pastime in Cuba.

The second book was *Hidden History of Mobile* (The History Press, 2020.) This was a fun book to write because it allowed me to dig beneath the surface of the city's everyday history and bring to life some lesser-known and forgotten stories of the city's past.

It was at this point in my writing career that an idea came to me to introduce the rich history of Mobile to travelers, vacationers and even residents of the city who may not know how vibrant their city's past was. I envisioned it being a travel guide, if you will, to Mobile and the Alabama Gulf Coast's past. The goal was for the book to be an introduction to the area's history but with a twist—guiding readers to see the history and experience it firsthand. Thanks to Joe Gartrell and The History Press, I was afforded the chance to do just that, and here we are.

The history of Mobile begins well before the first Europeans established the initial fort that would become Mobile atop a high bluff—Twenty-Seven Mile Bluff—overlooking the Mobile River in 1702. It begins during an archaeological period of time known as the Woodland Period, which occurred between 500 BC and AD 1000, when Native Americans roamed this landscape as hunter-gatherers but soon began developing utensils and weaponry as well as holding religious ceremonies.

During the Mississippian Period (from about AD 800 to AD 1600), Native Americans became more civilized and technologically skilled. It was during this period that we learn of the mound builders, who built tremendous dirt mounds by hand—some more than forty feet tall, one basket full of dirt at a time—atop which religious and tribal leaders would live and ceremonies would take place. From the top of these tall mounds, the leaders could look down on smaller secondary mounds and a plaza where the more common people of the chiefdom would live. Sadly, we will discover that the tribe for which the city was named, the Mabila, suffered brutally at the hands of early European settlers from Spain who came to the region in search of mythical gold and other treasures, as well as another enemy of the native peoples—yellow fever—that was brought to the New World by those same Europeans.

In the eighteenth century, the city proper began to take form as the French made their way into Mobile Bay, with the first settlement being established in 1702. Since that time, Mobile has seen and made some incredible history. It has survived the ravages of hurricanes and yellow fever epidemics. It was passed down from one country to another during its early history. As it became one of the major and richest seaports on the Gulf Coast, the city fell on economic tough times as the Union navy blockaded the bay and halted trading. The city also witnessed the last major battle of the Civil War, which was fought only miles away on the eastern shore of the bay, and was only spared the ravages of war when Generals Lee and Grant signed the document that virtually ended the war on the very same weekend.

The history of Mobile is sometimes tragic. It is here that the tale and legacy of slavery played out to its finale on the shores of Mobile Bay with the unbelievable story of the last slave ship, the *Clotilda*. That remarkable story is preserved to this day in the memories of the *Clotilda*'s descendants in nearby Africatown.

In contrast, the city's history is a celebration. As mentioned earlier, Mobile is recognized as the birthplace of Carnival and Fat Tuesday (Mardi Gras) in America.

As I said, my goal for this book is to be a travel guide to the history of Mobile and the surrounding areas of the Alabama Gulf Coast—both Mobile and Baldwin Counties. My desire is to tell you the history of the area and then, at the end of each chapter, take you to places where you can experience the history in that chapter firsthand. I call it "Your Guide to History." These sites include museums, but there are many more sites that you can physically touch and visualize the history outside the confines of museum walls.

I will take you to an island in the middle of absolute nowhere, but is in fact only a few miles from the city, to experience ancient Native American mounds. We'll visit centuries-old cemeteries with striking Victorian funerary, historic stone forts where one of the most famous American naval battles occurred and beautiful antebellum mansions where rows of live oak trees draped in flowing Spanish moss welcomes you. We'll pay a visit to a stone marker laid by a surveyor for George Washington in 1798 as a demarcation line between the southern boundary of the United States and Spanish Florida (which included Mobile) and visit the legacy of those who survived the voyage of the *Clotilda* at Africatown. And these are just for starters.

But how do you relate this incredible—and long—history in a coherent way without becoming too overwhelming? I have chosen to break the history down into eras, small nuggets that build one on top of the other, all interwoven to paint the complex picture of Mobile history.

It is not only Mobile history we will visit. The timeline also includes the other half of the Alabama Gulf Coast: Baldwin County. Located across the bay from downtown Mobile, Baldwin County has played a significant role in much of the history we will talk about.

The history I will present can get a bit complicated, especially when you throw in two other Gulf Coast cities—Pensacola, Florida, and New Orleans, Louisiana—both of which have their own stories, especially the early history in the early 1700s through the mid-1800s, that are intermingled. Just for perspective, and for those of you who don't already know this, Mobile (which is located almost dead center on the northern coast of the Gulf of Mexico) has Pensacola about 60 miles to its east and New Orleans 145 miles to its west, so I will be dropping the names of those two cities in many times throughout the book.

Now, keep in mind that Mobile, as compared to other Alabama cities that would eventually develop after the acquisition of the territory by the United States in the early 1800s, has a diverse population. The lineage of its residents runs deep—Native Americans, Europeans, Creole, African Americans and more—and the city is quite proud of this diversity. That diversity has allowed the city to see the world in a different light. As the Southern states were peeling away from the Union to begin the Civil War, there were many Mobilians who were not as quick to secede, realizing that their livelihoods and economy would be destroyed when the port would be blockaded by the North. The city also had the largest population of free Black people in the state. But don't get me wrong. It wasn't a utopia for people of color in the city. At the same time, attitudes toward Black and enslaved people still permeated throughout the population, forming a wide social gap between the haves and have nots.

Finally, realize that this is not a complete history of Mobile and the Alabama Gulf Coast. The stories and events of the region are, as I said, quite intricate, and I encourage you to review the selected bibliography at the end of this book to learn more.

Let us begin our journey through the history of this amazing American city, but before we head off to the past, let me introduce you to a few museums and tours that together make the perfect jumping-off points to begin your journey. These attractions will give you a good overview of the history of Mobile and the Alabama Gulf Coast.

Thank you for joining me on this journey.

YOUR GUIDE TO HISTORY

Mobile History Museum
111 South Royal Street, Mobile
(251) 208-7569
historymuseumofmobile.com
Admission: Fee

The entire history of Mobile and the Alabama Gulf Coast from ancient Native American artifacts through to the fight for civil rights in the 1960s is on display at the city History Museum of Mobile. The museum also rotates national exhibits as well. The History Museum is housed in the old Southern Market/Old City Hall, which was built in 1855.

Mobile Public Library Local History and Genealogy
753 Government Street, Mobile
(251) 494-2190
mobilepubliclibrary.org/locations/localhistory.php
Admission: Free

A wealth of knowledge is stored in the city's history and genealogy library— shelves of books, maps, photos and an extensive archive of newspapers on microfiche dating back to the early 1800s can be found here. It's free to browse, and you'll never know what you might uncover.

Daphne Museum
405 Dryer Avenue, Daphne
(251) 620-2600
daphneal.com/452/Daphne-History-Museum
Admission: Free; donations requested

The town of Daphne is located on the eastern shore of Mobile Bay, directly across from Mobile. Located in the second-oldest church in Baldwin County (the 1858 Daphne Old Methodist Church), the Daphne Museum presents a fascinating look at the history of the town and surrounding communities through artifacts and knowledgeable staff.

Built in 1855 as the city's Southern Market and first city hall, this building is now home to Mobile's history museum. *Author's collection.*

Fairhope Museum of History

25 North Section Street, Fairhope
(251) 929-1471
fairhopeal.gov/departments/museum
Admission: Free

Also located on Mobile Bay's eastern shore is the quaint town of Fairhope, where, through permanent and rotating exhibits, the Fairhope Museum of History presents the history of the town and the eastern shore of Mobile Bay. The museum is located in the Old City Hall, which was built in 1855.

Gulf Shores Museum

244 West Nineteenth Street, Gulf Shores
(251) 968-1473
gulfshores.com/things-to-do/gulf-shores-museum
Admission: Free

In a quite appropriate beach cottage, the Gulf Shores Museum along the Gulf of Mexico is a collection of exhibits focused on the maritime history of this Gulf Coast beach community in south Baldwin County.

Baldwin County Heritage Museum
25521 US 98, Elberta
(251) 986-8375
Admission: Free
facebook.com/BCHeritageM

With six large exhibit rooms in a twenty-thousand-square-foot building and covering five acres, the Baldwin County Heritage Museum is a journey back in time to the early days of Alabama's other Gulf Coast county, Baldwin. The museum focuses particularly on the farming history of the county that was vitally important to Mobile and the surrounding towns during the area's formative years.

Secret History Tour
(251) 752-9868
secrethistorytours.com
Admission: Fee

Take a fun and informative walk along the streets of Mobile with knowledgeable guides as they take you back through Mobile's three-hundred-plus-year-old history. A variety of tours will take you back to the city's pirate days, haunted locations, the earliest history of the city, Prohibition days and many more. Some tours begin with a snack and cocktail at downtown establishments.

ACKNOWLEDGEMENTS

O nce again, I have to thank the many people and organizations for their help in researching this book, obtaining photographs and generally keeping me on the straight and narrow. Thank you again to my wife, Maggie, for all of the help and support she gives during the harrowing months when a deadline is looming (I can be a bear). Thanks also to Dr. Greg Waselkov, author and Director of Historic Blakeley State Park Mike Bunn, the University of South Alabama Archaeological Museum, the Alabama Department of Archives and History and my friends at the Mobile Public Library Local History and Genealogy Library. Your guidance through the maze of resources is invaluable.

Chapter 1

THE FIRST MOBILIANS

THE WOODLAND AND MISSISSIPPIAN PERIODS

To tell the full story of the history of Mobile, we have to go back more than three thousand years to what archaeologists call the Woodland Period. This is the period of time between 500 BC and AD 1100, when Earth's climate was more moderate, perfect for habitation by the region's early Indigenous people.

Many Woodland Period sites have been discovered in and around the Mobile–Tensaw River Delta. Although small, these sites have given archaeologists and historians a glimpse into mankind's early existence near what is now present-day Mobile. Much of this evidence comes in the form of shell middens that can be found scattered about the area. One of the most notable is located on Dauphin Island at the Indian Shell Midden Park.

A midden—or in the case of those found along the coast, a shell midden—is basically a trash heap left behind by the early inhabitants of the Gulf Coast. It is from this "trash" that we can learn how these people once lived. Through these middens, archaeologists have found that people of the Woodland Period were frugal and didn't waste anything. Hides from animals were used to make clothing, and shells and bones were hewn into utensils.

The middens also indicated that the people of the period had a rich diet of not only big game such as deer and bear but also seafood pulled from the rich nutrient-filled waters of Mobile Bay and the Gulf of Mexico. The men would travel far from the camp to bring home the big game, while the women and children of the settlement would stay nearby and hunt for small game and seafood. Evidence from these middens show that they would cook clams over small open fires on small grills.

It wasn't until the Mississippian Period—more than one thousand years ago—that archaeologists could get a comprehensive picture of the later Indigenous people who lived in the Mobile region. This period saw the people who lived in the area move into a more agricultural way of life, where they added to their diet by growing beans, corn, squash, watermelon and pumpkins.

This period was known for its mound builders, who constructed towering hills made out of dirt and mud carried one basket at a time by hand by workers from borrow pits. The top of the mounds were flat and were topped with huts that had walls made of river mud and cane and palmetto frond thatched roofs, all of which were supported by wooden posts. These structures were occupied by the religious and secular leaders of the community, or "chiefdom," who could look down on their subjects in the cleared "courtyard" below.

A chiefdom is a form of social order where a single person exercises political and economic power over not just one but many communities. The mounds of the Mobile area were part of the Pensacola Chiefdom, which stretched from the Gulf Coast northward to present-day Selma.

Several mounds in a community were clustered together and were used for different purposes. Smaller mounds were used for religious ceremonies and rituals, while others were used as burial sites.

The greatest example of these mounds in the Mobile area is found deep in the dark and mysterious backwaters of the Mobile–Tensaw River Delta, the second-largest such delta in the country, where many streams and tributaries channel fresh water from a large expanse of the Southeast into an intricate system of bayous and backwaters only minutes from present-day downtown

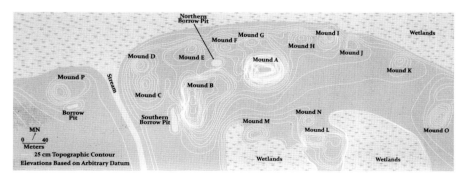

A map of the layout of the mounds on Mound Island found deep within the Mobile–Tensaw River Delta. *Author's collection.*

Mobile. These mounds, known as the Bottle Creek Indian Mounds, are located on a small island in the delta. Bottle Creek is the name of the dark water creek that rings part of the island. This complex of mounds is more commonly referred to as Mound Island.

Mound Island was a settlement with eighteen mounds, the tallest (called Mound "A") more than forty-five feet tall—quite an accomplishment seeing that it was built by hand one basket full of dirt at a time. Far below the top of the mound, the island, which is now overgrown with palmetto and vines, had a cleared plaza like a modern courthouse square where the citizens went about their daily lives, including playing games of skill like stickball and chunkey. Chunkey was a particularly challenging game in which a round stone disc called a "discoidal" is rolled across the ground, and where it stops, the warriors would throw spears at it. The closest spear to the stone wins. Many times, both men and women would place bets on the competitors and gamble material possessions on the games.

Being on an island in the middle of a labyrinth of bayous and channels, the Bottle Creek Indians were adept at boat building, which they used to create trade routes between villages. Huge cypress trees would be set on fire. When the trees finally fell, the log would be set on fire a second time, and the glowing bark would be scraped and hewn into a dugout canoe.

A trip to Mound Island is a fascinating journey back in time, and while you can travel to the island yourself by kayak, it is best visited via tour boat, where historians can show you what you are looking at and describe the history there (see the "Your Guide to History" section that follows). As mentioned earlier, the island has been reclaimed by nature, and the mounds are difficult to see. A historian will bring them to life in the thick forest. How thick is it? The delta is now called "America's Amazon," which gives you some idea. The one-mile trail to Mound "A" is lined with thick stands of palmetto and vines. It's a beautiful and unique walk to say the least.

Eventually, Europeans arrived in the northern Gulf of Mexico and came face to face with Native Americans, including the original Mobilians, the Mabila tribe, whose name was later anglicized to Mobile. While it is recognized that Spaniards first arrived in the area in the early 1500s (we'll discuss this in the next chapter), there is a tantalizing tale—a legend, actually—that puts Europeans on the shores of the Gulf of Mexico and what would become Mobile in the year 1170. From there, these early explorers of legend moved inland from Mobile Bay into the delta and beyond, where they themselves would contact more Native American tribes. Legend has it that these explorers weren't Spanish or French but Welsh.

Today, the mounds on Mound Island are hidden in the thick delta forest. This example of what one of the mounds would have looked like is from Moundville Archaeological Park in Moundville, Alabama. *Author's collection.*

A postcard from 1958 depicts a marker that was erected at Fort Morgan along Baldwin County's Gulf beaches to honor the legend of Prince Madoc of Wales' alleged arrival at Mobile Bay in AD 1100. *Curteich Color, "Prince Madoc Memorial Marker," Mobile Public Library Digital Collections, http://digital.mobilepubliclibrary.org/items/show/2357.*

The only trouble is that there is no evidence that backs up the legend. The story was first told by bards in Europe around crackling campfires and later put to paper by historians and poets of the sixteenth century. The story was also published in a book, *An Enquiry into the Truth of the Tradition Concerning the Discovery of America by Prince Madog ab Owen Gwynedd*, by Presbyterian minister John Williams in 1791. While it is just a legend, it is still a fascinating tale.

As the story goes, Prince Madog of Wales, one of many sons of King Owain Gwynedd, feared that he would be assassinated by his brothers, who were warring with each other following the death of their father. Madog and a group of followers climbed aboard an oak sailing ship and headed west into the Atlantic Ocean. And that's where history ends and legend begins. The story continues by claiming that Madog and his crew were blown off course into the Gulf of Mexico, where they sailed into what would become known as Mobile Bay. From there, they rowed boats north into the Mobile-Tensaw Delta and then up the Alabama River, where they first encountered Native Americans.

Later, when Europeans actually arrived in the New World and headed north from the coastal areas, they claimed to have encountered a group of natives with fair complexion and who spoke the Welsh language.

The only sign of this legend in Mobile is an old historic marker that stands behind Richards DAR House on North Joachim Street, hidden away because of the dubious nature of the story.

Whether the story was true or not, it was enough for Queen Elizabeth of England to lay claim to this new land in 1578, claiming that the legend proved that England had arrived hundreds of years before Columbus. She would send Sir Walter Raleigh across the ocean for what would be the Roanoke Virginia Expedition, an attempt to establish a British colony in Roanoke, Virginia. But it wasn't the British who began exploring and establishing settlements along the Gulf Coast. Fifty years prior to Britain's attempt to colonize the east coast of this new land, another European country, Spain, would be the first to explore Mobile Bay.

YOUR GUIDE TO HISTORY

Bottle Creek Indian Mounds

Delta Explorer, Historic Blakeley State Park, 34745 State Highway 225, Spanish Fort
(251) 626-0798
blakeleypark.com/Cruises
Admission: Separate fees for park and boat tour

The mounds are located on an island deep in the Mobile–Tensaw River Delta and are only accessible by boat. While you can kayak to the island (see the following for information on the Bartram Canoe Trail), paddling the delta is not for neophytes, with its plenty of alligators, snakes and confusing channels. It is best to visit with a tour guide who can show you the mounds hidden in the forest and describe the incredible history before you.

Bartram Canoe Trail: Everything you need to know about kayaking to the island can be found at the following website: alabamacanoetrails.com/bartram/indian-mound-island-trail.

Five Rivers Delta Resource Center

30945 Five Rivers Boulevard, Spanish Fort
(251) 625-0814
www.outdooralabama.com/activities/5-rivers-alabama-delta-resource-center
Admission: Free

Known as the "Gateway to the Delta," Five Rivers is a state-run facility located on the banks of Mobile Bay that brings the delta to life with educational displays examining the delta's unique environment and wildlife, plus its history. The facility also hosts many events with knowledgeable authors, historians and naturalists on a variety of subjects and has a theater where movies related to the delta and nature are shown throughout the day. Ask one of the staff to show you its catalogue, and depending on the crowd that day, they will be glad to queue it up for you.

Located in the middle of absolute nowhere, Mound Island is a registered national historic landmark. *Author's collection.*

Indian Shell Mound Park

1 Iberville Drive, Dauphin Island
(251) 861-5525
townofdauphinisland.org/things-to-do/indian-shell-mound-park
Admission: Free

Archaeologists from the University of South Alabama uncovered the shell ring mounds or midden on Dauphin Island and dated them back to the Mississippian Period. It is a nice little park with a small trail that meanders through the pines and oaks, with interpretive signage along the route.

MOWA Choctaw Cultural Center

1080 Red Fox Road West, Mount Vernon
(251) 829-5500
mowachoctawindians.com
Admission: Free

Three rooms—the Choctaw, Cherokee and Geronimo Rooms—display artifacts recalling the early days of the tribes in Mobile and Washington Counties. Visitation is by appointment only.

The small museum in this 1910 church in Orange Beach documents early Native American life on the Gulf Coast. *Author's collection.*

Orange Beach Indian and Sea Museum

25805 John Snook Drive, Orange Beach
(251) 981-8545
www.orangebeachal.gov/facilities/indian-sea-museum/about
Admission: Free, donation requested

Housed in a 1910 schoolhouse, the museum (which is located behind the Orange Beach City Hall complex) holds an eclectic array of Native American artifacts from the Gulf Coast region, including a dugout canoe as well as a collection of maritime-related displays. The museum is open Tuesday, Wednesday and Thursday 9:00 a.m. to 4:00 p.m.

Richards DAR House

256 North Joachim Street, Mobile
(251) 208-7320
www.richardsdarhouse.com
Admission: Fee

Besides touring the 1860 Italianate townhouse, step outside to the backyard to view the plaque dedicated to Prince Madog ab Owain Gwynedd, who (as legend has it) was the first European to sail into Mobile Bay in the year 1170.

Poorch Creek Indian Museum

5484 Jack Springs Road, Atmore
(251) 368-9136, ext. 2050
pci-nsn.gov/wordpress/about/museum-2
Admission: Free

A fascinating look at the history of the Poarch Creek Indians, including many artifacts—stoneware, pottery, tools and more.

University of South Alabama Archaeological Museum

6050 USA Drive South, Mobile
(251) 460-6106
southalabama.edu/org/archaeology/museum
Admission: Free; donation requested

The University of South Alabama's Archaeological Museum holds the definitive collection of artifacts that covers thousands of years of Mobile history, including an extensive collection and exhibits from the Woodland and Mississippian Periods.

Chapter 2

THE FIRST EUROPEANS ARRIVE

1519 TO 1698

The story of Mobile and the Alabama Gulf Coast as we know it begins with the arrival of the first Europeans during what is known as the Age of Discovery, a period of time between the years 1450 and 1650, when the great European nations began to spread their wings and set out to explore the far reaches of the world. Those voyages did not initially begin as a means of conquering land and claiming its treasure. Instead, they began as business ventures with countries searching for new trade routes to Asia.

The first European country to make an incursion into the Gulf and to what would be known as the New World was Spain. It was in 1493 that Christopher Columbus established the first Spanish settlement, Isabella, on the island of Hispaniola in the Caribbean. It was near this settlement that the colonists discovered vast fortunes in gold, shifting Spain's mission from one of trade to a thirst for the resplendent mineral—and that thirst was strong.

The Spanish conquest of the region began soon after, first taking Puerto Rico in 1508, Jamaica in 1509 and Cuba in 1511. The natives who called these islands home suffered mightily, either by being forced into servitude working in mines, being killed in droves during battles with the conquistadors or dying off in mass numbers due to another foreign invader—diseases that were introduced to the land by their conquerors.

Spain was the first to explore and lay claim to the entire crescent of the Gulf Coast of the New World from the tip of present-day Florida at Key West to Mexico, an area that they called "La Florida."

In 1519, the Spanish government commissioned conquistador and cartographer Alonso Álvarez de Pineda with exploring the North American Gulf Coast for passage to the Pacific Ocean. Pineda left Jamaica in March 1519 with four ships and became the first European to map the entire Gulf Coast. The explorer charted the existence of the many estuaries along the coast, including the Rio Grande and Mississippi River. He was also the first European to create a rudimentary chart of what would later be called Mobile Bay.

Pineda's voyage took him first to the Florida Panhandle on the northern Gulf Coast, where he turned and headed east and south in a futile attempt to prove the findings of a previous explorer, Ponce de Leon, who claimed that Florida was an island, not a peninsula, and that further exploration would prove easy passage from the Gulf of Mexico to the Atlantic Ocean. As Pineda soon discovered, de Leon was incorrect. The land mass was, in fact, a peninsula, which he verified upon his arrival at the southern tip just north of Cuba. Once he entered the straits between Florida and the Caribbean island, strong currents and winds forced him to turn around and sail back north along the west coast of Florida, eventually turning westward to explore the entire Gulf Coast crescent.

During the voyage, Pineda and his crew encountered many native tribes and marveled at the incredibly beautiful gold jewelry that adorned their bodies. Pineda wrote that the jewelry was "in their nostrils, on their ear lobes, and on other parts of their body." This description would lead to a devastating future in subsequent years for tribes across the Gulf Coast.

Next to arrive was Pánfilo de Narváez in 1528. Narváez was a ruthless conquistador who first arrived near what would later be Tampa, Florida, to begin an overland campaign with three hundred of his men to take the natives' gold. The crew brutally tortured and massacred the tribes they met along the way in an attempt to force them into relinquishing their treasure, but it was all for naught. The gold they sought was only a myth.

It didn't take long for word to spread among the Gulf's Native American villages about Narváez, and soon the expedition found itself under attack by tribes at every turn. By the time they had reached what would later be St. Marks, Florida, Narváez and his crew were a beaten lot. To make matters worse, the ships that were scheduled to meet the expedition and pick them up for a return trip home never arrived.

With supplies dwindling, the crew built five open boats from trees, stitched their clothing together to form sails and then proceeded westward to what would later become Pensacola, where the local tribe there promised to aid them with food and water. It was all a deception. In the middle of the night, the tribe attacked the Spaniards.

Narváez's remaining crew struggled farther west until they reached Mobile Bay, where they headed a short distance north up its wide mouth. En route, Native American scouts greeted the Spaniards and promised to provide them with food and water. To show that they were sincere in their offer, two of the Indians stayed with Narváez, while two of his crew, a Greek sailor named Teodoro and an unnamed Black crewmember, traveled with the scouts to secure the provisions.

As the sun was setting, the Indian scouts returned, but without Narváez's two crewmembers, and when the sun rose the next morning, Narváez and his men found themselves surrounded by and attacked by Indians. The crew barely made it out alive and continued sailing westward along the coast. One by one, the tiny boats were lost at sea, including the boat carrying Narváez. In the end, only four of Narváez's crew survived the disastrous expedition.

As mentioned earlier, during Spain's incursions inland from the Gulf Coast, they encountered many native tribes, one of which were the Mabila. The early explorers believed that the tribe was a "great empire" covering the entire central southeast region of the New World. Their language, Mabilian, was basically the English of the day for the tribes in the region and was spoken across the Southeast.

While early meetings between Spanish explorers and the Mabilians was cordial, later encounters was far from that, especially after the arrival of Hernando de Soto and his crew, who crisscrossed the southeast on a mission—the quest for El Dorado, or the legendary Lost City of Gold.

De Soto and more than six hundred troops arrived in the New World in 1539 and began moving north along the Florida peninsula. Along the way, his contingent of conquistadors stole food stores from the Native American villages they encountered and took their women. They would kidnap warriors to ensure their safe passage and use them to carry their supplies, as well as force them to guide his soldiers to other villages with every intention of locating and pilfering the gold they hungered for. Most of the time, these guides would mislead De Soto and take the men well off course to avoid the larger villages.

The following year, the expedition marched into what would later become Alabama near present-day Montgomery and began turning south. It was in this area where De Soto met the leader of the tribes of the area, Chief Tuscaloosa. The towering chief was described by one of De Soto's men as "an Indian so large that, to the opinion of all, he was a giant."

Once again, De Soto made his demands, but he did not know who he was dealing with. Tuscaloosa replied that he was not accustomed to serving anyone. Enraged, De Soto took the chief prisoner. The chief realized that he had no hope of dealing with the heavily armed Spanish, so he relinquished and promised to help De Soto supply whatever they needed at the village of Mabila.

The chief did, in fact, lead the expedition to Mabila, but De Soto wasn't expecting what greeted them. The village was small but had a strong palisade surrounding the compound of eighty buildings. Arriving before his army, De Soto and a few of his men entered and were entertained by twenty dancing girls.

An altercation between one of De Soto's men and a warrior lit the fuse, and thousands of Native Americans who were lying in wait cascaded out of the buildings and other hiding places. The Battle of Mabila would be the bloodiest to ever take place on North American soil between Europeans and Native Americans. When the dust had settled, the Spaniards had lost 20 men, with 250 wounded. The tribe, however, was devastated. Estimates

This beautiful painting titled *Discovery of Mobile Bay: Alonso Alvarez de Pineda Encounters the Mississippian Culture in Mobile Bay Circa 1518*, by artist Dean Mosher, hangs in the University of South Alabama Archaeological Museum. *Author's collection.*

have their losses between 5,000 and 6,000. Between the defeat at Mabila and the spread of diseases brought to the region by the Spaniards, the tribe was decimated. De Soto, who was wounded in the battle, never did find El Dorado and died after crossing the Mississippi due to fever in 1542.

The site of the Battle of Mabila has never been found. It was once believed to have been close to where present-day Mobile is located, but excavations have disproven that theory, with archaeologists currently looking in Clarke County, about one hundred miles north of Mobile. As they will tell you, whoever discovers the site will be the finder of what is now called the "Holy Grail of southern archaeology." But the memory of the Mabila Indians continues today; when the French arrived in 1702, they renamed the river, bay and the future city after them: Mobile.

It wasn't until 1558 that Spain set its sights on building a permanent settlement along the northern Gulf Coast. Explorer Guido de Lavazares was dispatched by King Phillip II to scout a suitable site for such a settlement. Eventually, Lavazares sailed into *Bahia Filipina*—Phillip's Bay, or what we now call Mobile Bay.

Lavazares was known for his detailed descriptions of his voyages, and his accounts of the bay painted it as almost being the Garden of Eden, calling it the "largest and most commodious bay":

> *In this bay and its environs there are many fishing grounds and shellfish, too....*[T]*here are many stands of pine of the sort that is* [readily] *worked and also the sort that makes masts and lateen yards. There are oaks with sweet acorns and ones with bitter acorns, hazelnuts, cedars, junipers, laurels, and small trees that yield a fruit like chestnuts. There are high red cliffs on the east side* [of the bay], *from which bricks can be made, and near them is stone for construction. On the western shore there are yellow and gray clays for making pottery....There are many birds, eagles, geese, ducks, partridges, and turtledoves. And* [there are] *deer in great numbers....Indians were seen, and large canoes...and fishing weirs, and in their shelters, there were corn, beans, and pumpkins.*

One would think that such a glowing report would make Mobile Bay the ideal location for establishing a settlement, but eventually, conquistador Tristan de Luna selected *Ochuse*, better known today as Pensacola, Florida. The original Pensacola village was short-lived, however, being abandoned for assorted reasons, including one hurricane that devastated the settlement in 1559.

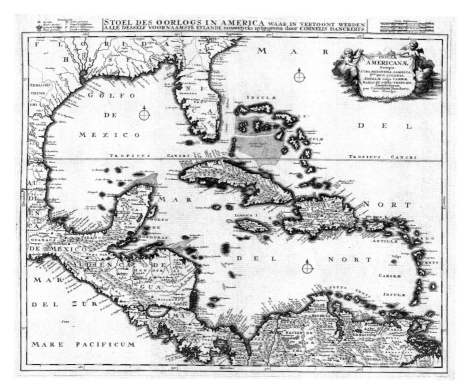

A stunning example of Cornelius Danckerts's 1696 map of Florida, the West Indies, Central America, the Caribbean and the Spanish Main.

With the exception of a few small and lightly manned forts near present-day St. Stephens (about an hour drive from Mobile) and Fort Nogales near present-day Vicksburg, Mississippi, Spain had virtually evacuated from the North American Gulf Coast. But even without any settlements of note, Spain still claimed the region as its own.

It wouldn't be until 1686 that Spain would return to Pensacola and reestablish the settlement. This time, it wasn't for conquering the land and natives or to search for mythical gold. It would be as a deterrent to the expansion of French colonialism that would see Mobile Bay become a key player in the geopolitical map of the northern Gulf Coast and see the birth of the city of Mobile. Eventually, Mobile would fall under Spanish rule during a period of time highlighted by a complex dance for ownership of the port city where it changed hands and flags several times.

YOUR GUIDE TO HISTORY

Spanish Fort

Sadly, the only remaining piece of the early history of Spanish settlements during this period is an earthwork that is on private property on Mobile Bay's eastern shore. The only vestige of Spain's early existence on the Alabama Gulf Coast is the town's name: Spanish Fort.

Spanish Plaza

401 Government Street, Mobile
Admission: Free

Although not related to Mobile's early Spanish history, the plaza does harken back to its Spanish past and honors its sister city—Málaga, Spain—with a beautiful fountain, sculptures and tilework from the country. There is, however, a statue in the plaza of Bernardo de Galvez, the man who led the Spanish capture of the city in 1780.

Spanish Plaza in downtown Mobile is a monument with flags, fountains and statues honoring the city's sister city—Málaga, Spain—and is a reminder of the city's Spanish heritage. *Author's collection.*

Chapter 3

THE MAKINGS OF A CITY

THE BIRTH OF MOBILE

By the mid-1600s, Spain was establishing colonies across the entire Florida peninsula and Mexico, but soon the Spaniards would have company: France.

In 1673, René-Robert Cavelier, Sieur de La Salle, set out from the city of Quebec on Lake Ontario to explore the Mississippi River from the north southward, reaching the Mississippi Delta on April 9, 1682. La Salle had with him a cross adorned with the French coat of arms emblazoned on it. He took the cross and planting it on the sandy beach, proclaiming, "I have taken and do now take possession…of this country, Louisiana."

Realizing the importance of Cavelier's discovery of the northern Gulf Coast, King Louis XIV dispatched several expeditions to explore and settle this new region, with the goal of establishing alliances with the native tribes who called the Gulf Coast home, seeking out natural resources for use at home in France and fostering the growth of these new settlements. The colonists were also instructed to conduct trade with Spain's Mexican territory. One of those expeditions was led by a pair of young French-Canadiens, Jean Baptiste Le Moyne, Sieur de Bienville, and his older brother, Pierre Le Moyne d'Iberville.

The brothers set sail to explore the Gulf Coast, and in February 1699, they established the first French settlement on the coast. They named it Fort Maurepas. In later years, the fort became synonymous with the local Native American tribes that inhabited the estuaries and backwaters, the Bylocchy, which was later anglicized to Biloxi. In three years, however, the fort would be abandoned, and Bienville and Iberville would be looking for a more suitable location to reestablish the settlement.

Continuing eastward, the expedition arrived at the mouth of Mobile Bay in 1700, landing on a small barrier island that Le Moyne d'Iberville named Massacre Island, so named because of the bleached human bones the expedition discovered on the island's beaches. Years later, his brother, Bienville, would rename the island Dauphine for the wife of the Duke of Burgundy. The name would later be anglicized to Dauphin Island.

Even though Spain had previously laid claim to the northern Gulf Coast, including Mobile Bay, all it had to show for it was a small settlement in Pensacola and several west of the Mississippi River. It did not see the potential of the bay and virtually left the territory open for expansion by other European nations, such as France. The French understood that the bay would be of critical importance in many ways. The dense forest was prime for logging, which would enable shipbuilding and the creation of forts. The abundant wildlife and marine life could provide food to sustain a settlement. Such a settlement in the area would serve as a bulwark against any incursions by the Spanish in Florida.

It also helped that there were friendly Native Americans who lived in the region, including the remnants of the Mabila tribe, a name that would be later anglicized to Mobile. The French realized that with a policy of diplomacy and not violence, they could establish a working relationship with the tribe and rely on them for trade to help make a new settlement successful, something that the early Spanish explorers never quite figured out.

Spain had overstayed its welcome with the tribes in the region after fighting many bloody battles with them, including the Mabila, over mythical gold that they believed the tribes possessed. The French, on the other hand, were more diplomatic and would eventually come to an agreement with the tribes: in exchange for food and assistance, the French would offer military assistance to protect the Mabilians from the Alibamu tribe with whom they were at war. As you may have guessed, the name of the state of Alabama was derived from Alibamu.

On January 10, 1702, Iberville dispatched Bienville from Massacre Island to head up the bay and Mobile River to establish a settlement close to the center of the Mabila tribe "sixteen leagues off at the second bluff." That "bluff" was located twenty-seven miles north of the island. The location was only twenty feet above the river's high-water mark, which Bienville believed would be high enough to escape river flooding. It was here that the

Plan of Fort Louis de la Mobile.
Mobile River. The Church (after contemporary map).

An early sketch of Fort Louis that would later move a little south on the Mobile River and become the city of Mobile. *Alabama Department of Archives and History.*

first settlement that would eventually become Mobile was established, *Fort Louis de la Louisiane*, also known as *Fort Louis de la Mobile.*

The fort's exterior consisted of four bastions that were made of double twelve-inch-thick logs. The bastions were backfilled with earth, and within that perimeter, housing, storehouses and a chapel were built. It is estimated that the fort could have held two to three hundred people in the event of an emergency. The entire structure would be encircled with a staked palisade. Behind the fort, about seventy residential houses were built.

With the completion of the new fort, the capital of fledgling French Louisiana was moved from Biloxi to Fort Louis de la Louisiane.

The early French settlers found life on the Mobile River to be harsh, with excessive high heat and humidity in the summer, hundreds of alligators lurking in the waters and squadrons of mosquitoes. To make matters worse, it wasn't only the early Spanish explorers who believed that there was gold to be found here. Many of the French colonists were also under the misconception that there were vast riches to be had along the bayous and backwaters and would rather dream of amassing a fortune in gold than work the land and grow crops in order to survive.

Bienville complained several times to the marine minister, Jean-Frederic Phelypeaux, Comte de Pontchartrain (an administrator for the new Louisiana colonies), about the idle colonists. In his letters, he warned that these men would be the downfall of the new French settlements. While the Native American tribes only had to barely scratch the ground, sow seeds and gardens would grow, the French colonists refused to even pick up a hoe.

Bienville also noted that the contingent of settlers, for the most part, were all men and asked how they could possibly create a sustainable population without "suitable" women: "If you want to make something of this country, it is absolutely necessary to send this year some families and a few girls who will be married off shortly after arrival."

The French government agreed and began recruiting women who were pious with impeccable virtue. They wanted women who had no family or prospects for the future. The Catholic Church was recruited to canvass convents throughout France to find women whose character was beyond reproach. The girls were promised a new life in a land of paradise and a chance to marry the brave French patriots in the new colony.

To be considered, a woman would need a letter of recommendation and then would have to go through a rigorous set of interviews to verify that they held the highest of moral values.

In October 1703, twenty-three young women ranging in age from fourteen to nineteen climbed aboard carriages along with escorts and traveled three hundred miles from Paris to Rochefort, France, where they would set sail on the three-month-long voyage aboard the vessel *Le Pelican* to the new French colony in Mobile. The girls were known by many names. Sometimes they were called *filles à la Cassette* or "cassette girls." Still others referred to them as *casquette* or "casket girls," a name derived from the small wooden box, a *casquette*, that the French government had given them containing a few essentials they would need to start life across the ocean. When the ship arrived in Mobile, they were known by the name of the ship they had sailed on and became the "Pelican girls."

Before arriving in the settlement, the ship, crew and passengers faced many perils. The *Pelican* nearly capsized in a massive storm off Haiti, and while in Cuba, they encountered mosquitoes, a small but powerful enemy that would play a huge role not only in the history of Mobile but also in the development of the entire Southeast of North America.

By the time the *Pelican* landed at Dauphin Island on August 1, 1704, those mosquito bites had taken their toll. Unbeknownst at the time, mosquitoes were the carriers of yellow fever. By the time the *Pelican* reached the island, half of the crew had died from the disease, as had several of the girls. After their arrival upriver at the settlement, numerous settlers and members of the Mabila tribe would also fall victim to the disease.

By 1720, the fort was in a sad state and was in complete disrepair. Additionally, Bienville and Iberville had underestimated the Mobile River and delta. As present-day Mobilians know all too well, the river and delta are prone to extensive flooding. It is the reason that the delta is such a fertile environment for wildlife and plants, as it sweeps its nutrient-rich water and sediment over its banks. For the settlement at Twenty-Seven Mile Bluff, that flooding was too much, and it had to be relocated, this time farther south away from the narrow river channel to the banks of the wider bay.

This engraving depicts the departure of "comfort girls," aka "Pelican girls" or "cassette girls" to the New World. *World Digital Library.*

Construction began on a new fort at what would become the site of present-day Mobile in 1723. Using plans drawn up by French military engineer Sebastian Le Prestre de Vauban, the fort would be a ten- to eleven-acre structure with the famous four-point star shape. The walls of the fort would be up to twenty feet tall and be made from locally fabricated bricks. Each star or bastion held a parapet on top, from which cannons and gunners could protect the fort.

Within the formidable fortress, two barracks, a bake house and a gun and ammunition magazine were built. The structure was built using slave labor, all of whom were removed from their homes in West Africa. The completed fort would be named Fort Conde in honor of the military leader during France's Wars of Religion, Prince de Conde. The fort would be the capital of the new French Louisiane territory.

Just prior to the construction of Fort Conde, Bienville established another settlement on the Gulf Coast on the first area of high ground that he found at the mouth of the Mississippi. It would be called Nouvelle Orleans, or New Orleans. Following a devastating hurricane in 1717 that destroyed the

A portion of the original Fort Conde is still visible near the re-creation of the fort on South Royal Street. *Author's collection.*

harbor at Dauphin Island, the capital was moved back to the original Fort Maurepas in Biloxi, and then five years later, in 1722, it was transferred once again, this time to New Orleans.

The French maintained control of these Gulf Coast colonies, including Fort Conde and the Mobile settlement, until 1763, when a newcomer sailed onto the scene and a great war broke out that saw Mobile and many other Gulf Coast settlements suffer from severe identity crisis as they changed hands between European countries not once but several times, through a dizzying array of treaties and conquests.

YOUR GUIDE TO HISTORY

Colonial Fort Conde

150 South Royal Street, Mobile
(251) 208-7569
historymuseumofmobile.com/colonial-fort-conde
Admission: Fee (included with admission to the History Museum of Mobile)

Built on the site of the original Fort Conde, the re-creation is a good representation of what the original fort once looked like. This re-creation was built in 1976 for the country's bicentennial and is about one-third the size of the original. Knowledgeable staff have a wealth of information about the fort's history and hold regular colonial firearm demonstrations, including cannon fire from a rampart.

The original Fort Conde has been lost to history, but a faithful re-creation (about one-third the original size) was constructed in 1976 where the original fort once stood. *Author's collection.*

Cooper Riverside Park/GulfQuest National Maritime Museum of the Gulf Coast

155 South Water Street, Mobile
Cooper Riverside Park: mobile.org/listing/cooper-riverside-park/737
GulfQuest Museum: gulfquest.org
Admission: Cooper Riverside Park—Free; GulfQuest—Fee

Described as a waterfront oasis in downtown Mobile, Cooper Riverside Park is a beautiful greenspace located on the banks of the Mobile River where you can take in the view of the river that made Mobile what it is today and experience its maritime history as you watch ships coming in and out of the harbor. The park also has magnificent statues of the city's French founders. Once you have taken in the waterfront, visit the GulfQuest National Maritime Museum of the Gulf Coast and experience the history of not only Mobile but the northern Gulf Coast as well.

Original Fort Conde

148 Church Street, Mobile
Admission: Free

The original Fort Conde was claimed by the rapid expansion of the city in the 1800s. During the construction of the Wallace Tunnel in 1966, remnants of the original fort were uncovered and are now on display on the south side of the city's Mardi Gras Park on Church Street.

Twenty-Seven Mile Bluff/Old Mobile

Historic Blakeley State Park Delta Explorer Cruises, 34745 State Highway 225, Spanish Fort
(251) 626-0798
blakeleypark.com/Cruises
Admission: Fee for boat tour

The only way you can visit the site of the original area of Fort Louis de la Louisiane on Twenty-Seven Mile Bluff is by taking one of the fascinating boat tours led by historian Mike Bunn. Contact the Delta Explorer Cruise at Historic Blakeley State Park for the latest schedule and prices.

Chapter 4

CHANGING PARTNERS

FROM FRANCE TO SPAIN TO THE "FOURTEENTH" COLONY

With the establishment of settlements in Mobile, Biloxi and New Orleans by the French in the early 1700s, Europe had secured a strong foothold and boundary lines for its acquisitions of territory in North America. In the Northeast, Great Britain was establishing its thirteen original colonies. Spain had New Spain, also known as the Viceroyalty of Spain, that basically consisted of Mexico, much of the southwestern United States and California, as well as the entire peninsula and panhandle of Florida, while France had established French Louisiana. Named for King Louis XIV, Louisiana was an expansive territory that encompassed most of the Mississippi drainage basin from the Great Lakes to the Gulf of Mexico and from the Appalachians to the Rocky Mountains.

Along the Gulf Coast, the ownership of Mobile Bay was always in dispute between France and Spain, but all-out war did not occur over the issue, at least not in the early 1700s. At the time, both Mobile (under French control) and Pensacola (under Spanish control) relied on each other for trade to sustain their settlements. The unofficial boundary between the two nations was the Rio Perdido, or Perdido River. The boundary became official with the signing of an accord between the two governments in 1719. That boundary still stands today as the state line between Alabama and Florida.

Hostilities eventually did boil over between the three nations in what Winston Churchill would call centuries later the "first world war." It was a war that would span five continents over seven years, hence the name the

Seven Years' War, or, as it was called in North America, the French and Indian War.

The three countries had been fighting small skirmishes over the years in North American in an attempt to expand their territory. In 1754, things came to a head when a young twenty-two-year-old George Washington was dispatched by the British to warn France not to encroach on the colony's westernmost boundary near Pittsburgh. The French refused, a skirmish ensued and a French ensign, Joseph Coulon de Jumonville, was killed.

The war was on. In North America, the French were aided by their allies, the Native American tribes with whom they had established trade relations. Spain, meanwhile, saw an opportunity to put an end to British expansion on the continent and threatened to declare war on Britain. In retaliation to the threat, Britain's King George III declared war on Spain on January 4, 1762.

Despite such a strong alliance between France and Spain on the Gulf Coast, Britain's military and naval strength was overwhelming. The war ended on February 10, 1763, with the signing of the Treaty of Paris. While the treaty was a patchwork of land swaps in the Caribbean, for the North American Gulf Coast—and Mobile in particular—it meant that the city was now under British rule. The treaty ceded all of French Louisiana from the Mississippi River westward to the Rocky Mountains (excluding New Orleans, which remained in French hands) to Spain, while the British picked up much of Canada and all land east of the Mississippi, including all of Florida and Mobile.

Britain split the former French and Spanish territories along the Gulf into two pieces: East Florida, which included the entire peninsula east of the Apalachicola River, and West Florida, which stretched from the Apalachicola to the Mississippi River. Mobile was now formally under British rule and was part of West Florida. It could be argued that at this time, Britain now had fifteen colonies in North America, of which Mobile was a part, and not just the original thirteen.

British rule over Mobile didn't last long, however, for in a mere twelve years, British colonists in the original thirteen colonies would revolt against British rule and taxes that were being heaped on them as a way for the monarchy to pay its debts from the French and Indian War. The Revolutionary War began on April 19, 1775. The Revolution opened the door for Spain, giving it a chance to regain its territory on the Gulf Coast, plus a little more, with a battle that occurred in Mobile Bay, the Siege of Mobile.

During the Revolution, France allied itself with the British colonists who were in revolt. In 1779, Spain allied itself with France and saw its chance to retake British-held forts along the Mississippi River, Mobile and then Pensacola.

The Revolution arrived on the Gulf Coast in January 1780 when Spanish governor Don Bernardo de Galvez quickly moved a small force of ships up the Mississippi River and captured the British posts there in a virtually bloodless campaign.

Galvez then moved his fleet of a dozen ships and eight hundred troops toward Mobile Bay. Upon arriving at the mouth of the bay, severe weather whipped up fierce winds and currents and grounded six of his ships on sandbars. Sailing the remaining ships north into the bay, Galvez established a base camp on Dog River that feeds the bay. He was soon reinforced with five ships and hundreds more troops from Havana. The Spanish shallow-draft ship the *Valenzuela* made its way to within two miles of Fort Conde (which, by this time, had been renamed Fort Charlotte by Britain) and opened fire on February 26, 1780.

By the end of March, Galvez and his men had established a battery only two thousand yards from the fort and thought it was time to take control. Galvez sent an emissary to the fort, where he met with Fort Charlotte's commander, Captain Elias Durnford. As the emissary discovered, the fort was in a sad state of repair and was only being manned by three hundred soldiers. He stressed to Durnford that he was outnumbered and that a battle would be futile, but Durnford refused to surrender:

> *The difference of numbers I am convinced are greatly in your favor, Sir, but mine are much beyond your Excellency's conception, and was I to give up this fort on your demand, I should be regarded as a traitor to my king and country.*

On March 12, Galvez sent the order to open fire. Two of the fort's walls were blasted apart, and several British cannons were destroyed. The British quickly ran out of ammunition, and by the time the smoke cleared, only one soldier on the Spanish side had died. As the sun set over the fort and Mobile Bay, the white flag of truce was raised over Fort Charlotte. Mobile was now under Spanish control.

With the victory, Galvez turned his eyes toward overrunning the British at Pensacola. His goal was delayed by a hurricane. While he waited out the storm, Galvez feared that the British would pursue a counterattack on Mobile after their devastating loss. As a precaution, Galvez ordered his

A view of Mobile Bay and present-day Mobile from Village Point Park Preserve in the area where the Village once stood. *Author's collection.*

men to construct a small fort on the eastern shore of Mobile Bay that they called the Village.

The eastern shore was important to Mobile in that it was of agricultural significance. The shore was lined with plantations that grew a variety of crops and, most importantly, had a small concentration of cattle farms that supplied the settlement with beef.

Archaeologists believe that the actual fort was located somewhere in the vicinity where Interstate 10 currently crosses the bay into the town of Daphne. It was a small wooden stockade with a few buildings surrounded by trenches and was manned by 190 men.

As Galvez predicted, British general John Campbell ordered two frigates to sail to Mobile and retake the city. On January 5, 1781, the ships raised false colors, fooling a small Spanish garrison stationed on Dauphin Island, and were able to easily land on the island, where they would secure some of the local's cattle for their own use. The Spanish weren't fooled for long, however, and opened fire on the invaders, forcing them to flee and continue sailing north.

Meanwhile, a contingent of British soldiers were making their way across land from Pensacola through thick maritime forests, wetlands and bogs toward the Village. They arrived at the fort on January 7 completely undetected. With fixed bayonets, the attack began.

The men manning the fort were caught by surprise but quickly regrouped and began to return fire. A British officer, Benjamin Baynton, later described the battle in a letter to his brother: "One continual sheet of fire presented itself for ten minutes. You may judge the gallantry of the officers when you read in the papers that out of ten, six were killed and wounded. It was Bunkers Hill in miniature."

Despite being taken off guard, the Spanish defense held and Spain retained the Village. In the end, there were thirty-two dead (eighteen British) and eighty-three wounded (sixty British).

When the Revolutionary War ended in 1783, British rule in North America was over. Spain once again controlled its original territory in East Florida but now was in complete control of West Florida and Mobile. The territory west of the original thirteen colonies, now the United States of America, became known as the Mississippi Territory. A line of demarcation was needed to delineate the border between the new country and Spain.

In 1796, President George Washington assigned Major Andrew Ellicott the task of surveying and marking this boundary. In 1799, Ellicott arrived at the 31st parallel, just twenty miles north of Fort Conde, and placed a large sandstone marker. On the north side of the marker (the U.S. side), the words "U.S. Lat 31 1799" (the parallel line and year) were inscribed. On the south side (the Spanish side), similar words were inscribed except in Spanish: "Dominos de S.M.C. Carolus IV. Lat 31 1799" (Dominion of his Catholic Majesty Charles IV).

Mobile was securely in Spanish hands, and the border between the two countries in North America had been established. But there were more battles to come, and Mobile would change hands two more times in the years to come.

YOUR GUIDE TO HISTORY

Ellicott Stone Historical Park

Alabama Highway 13, Axis; GPS coordinates: 30.996144, -88.025296
asce.org/about-civil-engineering/history-and-heritage/historic-landmarks/ellicott-stone
Admission: Free

The actual sandstone marker laid by engineer Andrew Ellicott can be found only 9.5 miles north of I-65 exit 19 on Alabama Highway 13 in Axis, Alabama. The park is a small pull-off from the highway. From there, you will see a sign that points in the direction of the stone. It is a short quarter-mile walk through the woods to the protective awning that covers the stone and the fence that keeps it safe from vandals. Overall, the hike is easy; however, it is in the woods, so use caution and watch your step. You will have to cross a set of railroad tracks on the way. Be very careful and watch for trains entering the nearby chemical plant.

Perdido River

Robertsdale, Alabama, off County Road 112; trailhead coordinates: 30.657833, -87.404500
5 Rivers Delta Resource Center
(251) 625-0814
alabamacanoetrails.com/perdido/hiking-trail; outdooralabama.com/activities/5-rivers-alabama-delta-resource-center
Admission: Free

Feel what it was like in 1719 when the Perdido River was the border between France and Spain. Today, the black-water river (it's actually tea color due to the tannin from the trees that line its banks) winds its way to the Gulf of Mexico. The banks are dotted with brilliant white sandbars, and the river itself is perfect for a swim on a hot summer day. The Perdido River Hiking Trail is the best way to experience the river. It is a 17.9-mile trail, but a nice 3-mile out-and-back hike to the first large sandbar gives you a feel for the environment as it was back then. The hike takes you through a beautiful Atlantic white cedar bog. Do not attempt to hike the trail after heavy rain or if a storm is approaching. The river floods and inundates the trail. Contact the 5 Rivers Delta Resource Center in Spanish Fort for full details of the hike.

Left: Only a short quarter-mile walk from a parking area on U.S. 43 in north Mobile County in the town of Axis leads to the Ellicott Stone, the border between the U.S. Mississippi Territory and West Florida (and Mobile) in 1799. *Author's collection.*

Below: The Perdido River that now forms the border between Alabama and Florida looks the same as it did in 1719, when it was the border between France and Spain in the New World. *Author's collection.*

Laced with history dating back to prehistoric times, French plantations and a historic French cemetery, Village Point Park Preserve in Daphne is a glimpse back in time to 1719 and the Village. *Author's collection.*

Village Point Park Preserve

27710 Main Street, Daphne
(251) 621-3703
villagepoint.info/vpwp
Admission: Free

Located on the eastern shore of Mobile Bay, the largest park in the town of Daphne, Village Point Park Preserve is the location of an amazing estuary teeming with plants, birds and alligators; gorgeous views of Mobile Bay and downtown Mobile from a sandy island; and plenty of history. Visit the enormous Jackson Oak, where some historians believe General Andrew Jackson gathered his troops before heading to the Battle of New Orleans in 1815, and a cemetery dating back to the late 1700s. Many of the tombstones are inscribed in French, harkening back to the area's first residents from Europe. The preserve is near the site of where it is believed the battle of the Villages occurred in 1780.

Chapter 5

BECOMING AMERICAN

A s the dust from the Revolutionary War settled over Mobile in 1783, the boundary lines between the newly formed United States of America and the Spanish territory of Florida along the Gulf Coast had to be formalized. For Mobile, that boundary was set at the 31st parallel, with the Ellicott Stone making it official.

Things became a little more complicated when, in 1802, Spain's King Charles IV signed a decree that transferred all of its territory west of the Mississippi River back to France. U.S. access to the river, the port of New Orleans and the Gulf of Mexico—all of which were of vital importance to the newly minted country for trade with Mexico and the Caribbean islands—was effectively cut off. The country couldn't even access the Gulf through Mobile since East and West Florida were still under Spanish control.

One year later, in 1803, the United States completed the Louisiana Purchase with France, which increased the size of the country by 827,000 square miles. After the sale, many in the United States believed that West Florida and Spanish Mobile were now actually U.S. territories, which they were not. They were not part of the deal, so in 1804, new boundary lines had to be established.

In 1804, President Thomas Jefferson appointed a young judge by the name of Harry Toulmin to the position of Superior Court judge for the Tombigbee District of the Mississippi Territory. The Mississippi Territory encompassed land that was recently acquired by the United States that stretched from the Mississippi River eastward to Georgia and from a line near where Alabama's future capital, Montgomery, would later be established to the 31st parallel that was demarcated by Andrew Ellicott in 1799. That demarcation line at the 31st parallel put Mobile only a short twenty miles away from the new country.

This block of land that the United States now controlled, the Mississippi Territory, was virtually landlocked, with Spain still in control of the Mississippi River and the Gulf Coast. Needless to say, colonists in the new territory desperately needed access to the Gulf of Mexico for trade to sustain their settlements.

The newly appointed Judge Toulmin was a supporter of the notion that the Gulf Coast areas should be annexed into the United States. The judge petitioned Congress to do just that, but his request was denied. Accepting Congress's decision, he officially set up his office in the territory on the 31st parallel at what was called Fort Stoddert, a stockaded fort with blockhouses located at the structure's four corners. The fort was named for the United States' first secretary of the navy, Benjamin Stoddert.

With his office right on Spain's doorstep, Toulmin set out on a mission—to keep Mobile in the hands of Spain until the United States decided it was time to annex the area.

Fast-forward to 1807 when rumors began to spread throughout the Mississippi Territory and Spanish Mobile that Aaron Burr—hero of the American Revolution, former vice president of the United States and the man who killed Secretary of the Treasury Alexander Hamilton in a duel—was coming to Mobile. Rumor had it that he was coming to the city with every intention of annexing the Spanish territory—*not* into the United States, though, but into a new and independent republic, which would be an act of treason as far as the United States was concerned.

Burr was a law student who became a twice-decorated war hero during the Revolution, once for saving the lives of an entire brigade of soldiers trapped in Manhattan by British troops and again for squelching a potential mutiny by George Washington's troops, who were facing an extreme northeastern winter at Valley Forge.

After the war, Burr completed his law degree and began a career in politics. He was elected to the New York State assembly twice, was appointed to the state's attorney general position and was then elected to represent New York in the U.S. senate.

In the 1800 presidential election, Burr ran against Thomas Jefferson and John Adams for the presidency. In the early years of the nation, candidates did not run on a ticket of president and vice president. Instead, all candidates vied for the presidency, with the runner-up becoming vice president.

Burr tied with Jefferson for office of president. The outcome of the election would be determined by the House of Representatives. Then Representative Alexander Hamilton began a blistering propaganda campaign against Burr in an effort to keep him out of office, which it did. Jefferson became president, and Burr was the vice president. But it wasn't a healthy working relationship, as Jefferson virtually ignored his vice president. He would often leave Burr out of important discussions and decisions. When Jefferson came up for reelection, Burr lost his position as vice president.

Now out of office, Burr made a run to be New York's governor, but once again, Hamilton made an appearance, publicly calling Burr "the most unfit and dangerous man of the community." The smear campaign was effective, and Burr suffered a devastating loss to Morgan Lewis. Burr couldn't take it any longer and called out Hamilton's smear campaign publicly. His resentment and hatred of Hamilton grew until, finally, he ended the dispute once and for all by challenging Hamilton to a duel. On the morning of July 11, 1804, the two met in a field in Weehawken, New Jersey, with Burr exacting his vengeance and killing Hamilton.

Burr's story picks up three years later on a cold February night in Mobile. A young Mobile lawyer, Nicholas Perkins, was spending the evening in a cabin near Fort Stoddert playing backgammon with a friend when the men heard the sound of approaching hoof beats. Then came a knock at the door.

Perkins opened the door and was greeted by a pair of travelers, one of whom he described as wearing ragged pants but also "strikingly beautiful boots." The cabin's crackling fire in the fireplace gave Perkins a glimpse of the face of the man who stood before him. Perkins noted that it was a noble face with "sparkling eyes."

The travelers asked directions to the nearest tavern and received them; thanking Perkins, they rode off. Perkins had heard the rumors and knew that Burr was wanted for treason. It suddenly dawned on him, and he turned to his friend and said, "That is Aaron Burr. I have read a description of him and I cannot be mistaken."

Perkins saddled his horse and galloped off into the night to get the sheriff. The pair made their way to the tavern, where they found the traveler and confronted him. The sheriff looked at the man and was not as convinced as Perkins that this was Aaron Burr, but after a lengthy conversation, the sheriff became a believer. Borrowing a canoe, the sheriff paddled down the Mobile River to Fort Stoddert, where he convinced the fort's commandant, Captain Edward P. Gaines, to put together a detachment of soldiers and arrest Burr.

At this point, there are different versions of the story about who exactly arrested Burr. One of those says that the following morning, the detachment from Fort Stoddert, led by Gaines himself, met up with the travelers. Gaines stepped up and asked, "I presume, Sir, I have the honor of addressing Colonel Burr?"

The traveler replied, "I am a traveler in the country and do not recognize your right to ask such a question."

Gaines continued talking with the man, and the more they spoke, the more he became convinced that this was Aaron Burr. He announced, "I arrest you at the instance of the Federal Government."

Burr calmly replied, "You are a young man and may not be aware of the responsibilities which result from arresting travelers on private business."

"I am aware of the responsibilities," Gaines said. "But I know my duty." And with that, Burr was arrested and held at Fort Stoddert, where his charm made him a popular prisoner with both the soldiers and settlers. He played chess with Judge Toulmin's daughter and even gave aid to Gaines when he became severely ill with stomach pains.

Another version of the story said that the detachment, and not Gaines, arrested Burr and suggested that Burr first met the commandant later in the day. According to this account, it is said that Burr was taken to the fort, where he walked into the commandant's room, where he was recuperating from stomach pain. Burr brought into the room a vial of medicine that he was going to offer Gaines to help ease the pain. As he walked into the room, Burr said, "I am Aaron Burr and a prisoner here, captured yesterday while going to Mobile. As soon as I can have a hearing, the infamous charges trumped up against me will fail. In the meantime, while compelled to remain within these walls, let us try to make our time pass as pleasantly as possible."

Whichever story is the truth, the story ends the same. One month later, Burr was turned over to federal authorities and tried for treason, but the prosecution could not find a single witness to prove that he had committed treason against the country and he was set free. Mobile never did become an independent country, but it would not remain a Spanish possession for long. But before Mobile would become part of the United States, a horrific massacre would take place across the bay that helped light the fuse for what would be a tragic event in American history, the Trail of Tears, and would see the Mobile area's Gulf Coast take on British troops not once but twice during the War of 1812.

Following the American Revolution, the bond between the newly formed United States and the Creek Indian nation was strengthened when a treaty between both parties was signed in New York in 1790. Immediately upon signing, U.S. Indian agent Benjamin Hawkins began implementing a series of programs designed to improve the Creeks' way of life, especially in the area of agriculture.

By 1812, a split had erupted within the Creek Nation, separating them into two factions. While one group embraced the alliance between the Creeks and Americans, the other, the Red Sticks or Upper Creek, believed in Indian nationalism and feared the growing expansion of white settlements into the South and cooperation between the tribe and the federal government. Their answer was to kill any Indian who allied themselves with the Americans and began to work on reforming the Creek culture to remove any commercial and American influences.

Tensions between the two groups grew until 1813, when a leader of the Red Sticks, Peter McQueen, negotiated a deal with the Spanish governor of Pensacola and acquired guns and almost three hundred pounds of gunpowder and lead shot. It was obvious that the Red Sticks would use force to confront Creeks, who they deemed too accommodating to the Americans.

On the way to acquire the arms, the Red Sticks burned the plantations of fellow Creeks. Hearing of the decimation of the plantations, Colonel James Caller of the Mississippi Territory Militia gathered 180 men, which included allied Creeks, and intercepted the Red Sticks at Burnt Corn Creek in present-day Escambia County, Alabama. Despite being caught off guard, the Red Sticks drove the militia out; the Battle of Burnt Corn Creek, the first of the Creek Indian Wars, was over, but the war had begun.

Fearing retaliation, families along the Tensaw and Tombigbee Rivers that feed Mobile Bay began building small fortresses for protection. Their fears were realized on August 30, 1813, when seven hundred Red Sticks led by William Weatherford attacked one of those forts, Fort Mims. The fort was located at present-day Stockton near Bay Minette in Baldwin County. It was a brutal massacre of men, women and children who had gathered in the small wooden fortress for protection. The Red Sticks had easily breached the fort's protection through an open gate.

Above: An engraving of a painting depicting the massacre at Fort Mims on August 30, 1813. *Alabama Department of Archives and History*.

Opposite: A pen-and-ink drawing of the plans for a new American fort at Mobile Point. The fort would become known as Fort Bowyer. *Barthélémy Lafon and U.S. War Department, Office of the Chief of Engineers, Plan of the Fortification at Mobile Point, 1813, https://www.loc.gov/ item/2012588004*.

The ensuing battle lasted five hours, and when it was over, more than five hundred had died on both sides. News of the slaughter spread quickly across the country, and the aftermath resulted in a number of battles between the tribes and the U.S. military, culminating in the Battle of Horseshoe Bend just northeast of the future state capital, Montgomery, and the beginning of the relocation of Native Americans from their land during the tragic Trail of Tears.

Meanwhile, as the United States was battling Native Americans and the British during the War of 1812, news arrived that Spain had evacuated Mobile. In April 1813, Colonel General James Wilkinson and his troops moved in quickly to take control of the city, including Fort Carlota (Spain had renamed Fort Conde yet again), Mobile Bay and present-day Baldwin County, thus opening access to the Gulf of Mexico.

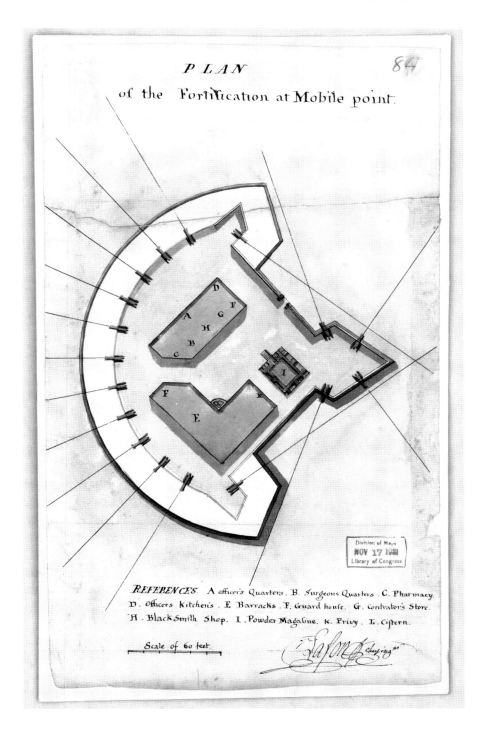

Wilkinson's men quickly built a redoubt on the tip of the beaches of a peninsula on the eastern side of Mobile Bay called Mobile Point that delineates the end of the bay from the Gulf of Mexico. By June, the troops had turned the redoubt into a proper fort that was about twenty-two thousand square feet in size with a four-hundred-foot semicircular wall.

The news of the bloodless capture of Mobile was received with great excitement, but it came with a warning. In the May 26, 1813 edition of the *Daily National Intelligencer*, there was an ominous report that there could be danger on the horizon from those "who might be hovering off the coast." That danger would be in the form of King George III's Royal Navy.

The War of 1812 began when Britain attempted to restrict U.S. trade. While devastating battles waged in the northern states, in the South, Britain sought to regain control of Mobile with the ultimate goal of taking New Orleans and cutting it off from trading with the East Coast. The plan was that the British would take Mobile Bay and the city where troops would disembark and march west to New Orleans. To take the bay, they first had to take out the new fort at Mobile Point, which by now had been named Fort Bowyer for its first commander, Colonel John Bowyer.

After occupying Spanish-held Pensacola, the British began preparing for the attack on Fort Bowyer. The United States, meanwhile, re-garrisoned the fort with 160 men from the Second U.S. Infantry under the command of Major William Lawrence. On September 12, 1814, Royal Navy captain William Percy sent a battalion of 225 royal marines and Native Americans nine miles east of the fort on the narrow, sandy peninsula. Two days later, the troops attacked the fort by land, while off the coast, the HMS *Hermes*, HMS *Sophie*, HMS *Caron* and HMS *Childers* moved into position with sixty-eight cannons. The only two British ships that were able to fire on the fort were the *Hermes* and *Sophie*.

After two hours of cannon volley, the *Hermes* ran aground directly underneath the gun ports of the fort, forcing Percy to scuttle the ship, and after being rescued by the *Sophie*, the captain called off the attack. The Americans had won a decisive battle against the Royal Navy, with seventy casualties tallied on the British side.

The Royal Navy changed plans and went on to directly attack New Orleans, but after a crushing defeat, it turned around for a second try at Fort Bowyer. General Andrew Jackson ordered that the garrison at the fort be increased to 375 men, with an additional twenty-eight cannons.

The attack began on February 7, 1815, but this time, Percy and his ships began the campaign with heavy bombardment of the fort. The following day, General Lambert marched a contingent of men from a position seven miles east of the fort to the fort's gates, where they established a siege line.

Major Lawrence and his men defending the fort held out for five days under intense bombardment before finally surrendered to Percy. The battle was in vain, however. Before the British could set sail and take over Mobile, the Treaty of Ghent was signed, thus ending the War of 1812. The British withdrew from the peninsula, and the fort reverted back to the Americans.

You have to remember that long after the War of 1812 had ended, the United States was in control of Mobile and West Florida and not East Florida (the Florida Panhandle and peninsula). In July 1821, Andrew Jackson was fully expecting that Spain would relinquish West Florida to the United States. Jackson's wife, Rachel, had even moved to Pensacola, while Jackson was moving his troops toward the city with every expectation of the region being turned over to the Americans.

After a long, drawn-out process of negotiations, Spanish governor Jose Cavalla ironed out the details of the agreement, and on July 17, 1821, Mobile as well as all of Florida officially became territories of the United States. Rachel Jackson described the moment when the transfer occurred to her friend Eliza Kingsley:

> At length, last Tuesday was the day. At seven o'clock, at the precise moment, they hove in view under the American flag and a full band of music. The whole town was in motion. Never did I ever see so many pale faces. I am living on Main street, which gave me an opportunity of seeing a great deal from the upper galleries. They marched by to the government house, where the two Generals met in the manner prescribed, then his Catholic majesty's flag was lowered, and the American hoisted high in air, not less than one hundred feet.

Mobilians were now officially Americans, and a new era was about to begin in the port city.

YOUR GUIDE TO HISTORY

Fort Bowyer Plaza/Battery
Fort Morgan Historic Site, 110 Highway 180, Gulf Shores
(251) 540-5257
fort-morgan.org
Admission: Fee

The actual fort where the two battles with the British took place in 1812 no longer exists, but a special monument has been erected at the site within the walls of the Fort Morgan Historic Site. There is also a World War II–era cement battery located here named Battery Bowyer that once protected the Gulf Coast from possible German invaders. It, too, was named for the fort's original commander.

Fort Mims
1813 Fort Mims Road, Stockton
(251) 533-9024
ahc.alabama.gov/properties/ftmims/ftmims.aspx
Admission: Free

A unique reproduction of the fort where the massacre at Fort Mims occurred. The area is dotted with interpretive signs to guide you through the horrific battle. There are reproductions of the fort's walls and blockhouse. The best time to visit is the last weekend of August, when volunteers hold a living history weekend and reenactment. There is an admission fee charged for the reenactment.

Fort Stoddert Marker
County Road 96, Mount Vernon; GPS coordinates: 31.091250, -87.981467
hmdb.org/m.asp?m=149312
Admission: Free

The original Fort Stoddert, the southernmost outpost of the newly formed United States of America in the Mississippi Territory, no longer exists, long since reclaimed by nature, but a series of interpretive signs tell the story of the fort along the banks of the Mobile River in north Mobile County.

A reproduction of the Fort Mims stockade, where the bloody massacre of 1813 occurred and ushered in the tragic Creek Indian War and the Trail of Tears. *Author's collection.*

Chapter 6

ANTEBELLUM MOBILE

U p to this point in the timeline of Mobile history, the "city" could still be called more of a settlement. In 1760, the population growth of the city was slow. At this time, it was still a backwater outpost along the Gulf Coast. In many areas, agriculture was difficult due to the sandy soil. And the bay, though wide with several navigable rivers leading northward like tentacles on an octopus, was shallow and not suitable for large ships to sail the relatively short distance north from the Gulf to the site of Fort Conde. To get to the settlement, larger ships would have to lighten their load by transferring cargo to a lighter boat (a shallow-draft boat or barge) to reduce its draft or face running aground.

In terms of population, in 1760, Mobile only had three hundred residents. By 1785, that number had grown to only seven hundred. At the turn of the century, things began to pick up. In 1809, the land on the east side of Mobile Bay was organized into a county, Baldwin County. Farming was a bit easier on that side of the bay, with a less sandy soil condition. Herds of cattle roamed fields, and with the acquisition of the settlement at Mobile by the United States following the War of 1812, Mobile County was established.

On December 17, 1819, only two days after Alabama officially became a state, the city of Mobile was officially incorporated and was immediately divided into seven wards, each to be represented by a member of the city's newly formed city council. From that moment on, the fortunes—and the population—of the city of Mobile began to grow.

This era from the end of the War of 1812 to the beginning of the Civil War became known as the "antebellum" period, a Latin word that literally means "before the war." It was a time when the economies of the North and South diverged greatly. In the North, the economy was based on industry, while in the South, cotton became king.

With the forced removal of Native Americans from their land and Alabama officially becoming a state on December 14, 1819, parcels of land not only in Mobile but across the state were ripe for the picking. Northerners and Europeans began purchasing land in droves and flocked to the state in what became known as "Alabama Fever."

While Mobile and Baldwin Counties had cotton farms, and still do to this very day, if you travel the backroads of both counties in early to late fall, when the white fluffy cotton balls bloom, it was the central and northern regions of the state where cotton farming was more prevalent. But what the Alabama Gulf Coast counties lacked in cotton fields, they more than made up for with several rivers (the Mobile, Alabama, Coosa, Tallapoosa, Tombigbee and Warrior) converging into Mobile Bay, which gave growers to the north direct access to the Gulf of Mexico, making transporting large shipments of cotton to the northern states and Europe relatively easy.

To give you an idea just how important cotton was to the economy of Alabama, the state produced 3.7 percent of the country's cotton in 1820. By 1849, that number had jumped to 22.9 percent, making Alabama the largest producer of cotton in the country. This also made the port of Mobile the second-largest exporter of cotton in the country, second only to New Orleans, and third-largest seaport overall in the country in terms of the total value of exports. This rapid growth, with cotton as the main economic driver for the state, came at the hands of enslaved Black men, women and children who deserve an upcoming chapter of their own.

During a visit to Mobile by British author Hiram Fuller, he described his first impression of the city: "Mobile—A pleasant cotton city of some thirty thousand inhabitants—where the people live in cotton houses and ride in cotton carriages. They buy cotton, sell cotton, eat cotton, drink cotton, and dream cotton. They marry cotton wives, and unto them are born cotton children."

An elite class was born out of this newfound wealth that held all of the economic and political power of the day—one that staunchly defended the system of forced slavery and set its own standards for gentility and honor while shaping what the roles of white men and women would be. A new societal class system was born.

With this economic boom, Mobile was on the move and growing exponentially as a prominent port city, but its status would soon be challenged by a rival—not from another state or country, but rather from the other side of Mobile Bay in Baldwin County.

Josiah Blakeley of Connecticut saw an opportunity to capitalize on Mobile Bay's eastern shore, where the Tensaw River had a much deeper channel than the Mobile River on the opposite side, allowing larger ships to sail into the bay. In 1814, the town of Blakeley was chartered.

The town had previously been a settlement for the Christian Apalachee tribe, whose members had converted to Catholicism and relocated to the site after the British destroyed their villages in Florida. Despite the massacre that occurred only a year earlier at Fort Mims to the north of this settlement, Blakeley was spared the ravages of the Creek Indian War and grew in prominence, rivaling Mobile as a major port city and shipbuilding center. In 1819, one year after the St. Stephens Steamboat Company sailed the first steam-powered vessel built in the state, the *Alabama*, down the Tombigbee River, shipbuilders in Blakeley had built the steamships *Tensa* and *Mississippi* on the bay.

The Mobile City Council saw the rise of Blakeley and realized that something needed to be done to keep the city's economy growing. With federal funding obtained through the backing of U.S. Senator Rufus B. King in Washington, the council added additional city money and began a project to widen and deepen the ship channel on the Mobile River, the first of many such projects over the next two hundred-plus years.

Blakeley, however, fell victim of its own design. The town was located at the entrance to the Mobile–Tensaw River Delta, and much of its shoreline was swamp. Mosquitoes carried a silent enemy that brought the town to its knees: yellow fever.

The disease is believed to have originated in Africa and was first brought into the New World by Columbus during his voyages in the 1490s. The disease flourished in the damp, humid subtropics of the Caribbean and the Gulf Coast. Hundreds of Blakeley's residents died from the disease, while others fled town in fear of the silent killer. No one knew at the time that the disease was carried by mosquitoes. Instead, the widely held belief was that the fever was brought on by the odor from the stagnant swamp waters that surrounded the town. By 1830, Blakeley was a ghost town and was being reclaimed by nature.

Back across the bay in Mobile, the city was entering a period that historians have called its golden age. The population was beginning to skyrocket to more than 3,194, making it the first official city in the state to be labeled an "urban center" in the 1830 census. Marshland along the riverbanks was filled in to build docks and warehouses, including the largest cotton warehouse in the city, built by William P. Hammond of Scotland. Hammond came to the city to build not only the warehouse but also the largest cotton press in Mobile.

Rows of docks were built and the original Fort Conde was razed in order to make room for new businesses. Banks and accounting firms began lining Commerce Street. Storefronts began springing up along Conti, Dauphin, Government, St. Francis and St. Michael Streets—all names that were throwbacks to the earlier French founding of Fort Conde. The local newspaper, the *Mobile Commercial Register* (the forerunner of the present-day *Mobile-Press Register*), was overflowing with ads for a variety of shops, including Roper and Moody's Fancy Retail Dry Goods and Store on the corner of Water and St. Francis and Wade Confectioners and Boarding House on Dauphin Street, where a full month of boarding cost fifty dollars with the bonus of having a full line of syrups, cordials and wine that could be "had at a moment's notice."

Hotels were established along Royal Street, the first being the Franklin House. The Franklin House was actually built in what was the state capital at the time, the town of Cahaba, and then floated down the Mobile River to Mobile in 1825 on a large flatboat before finding its final resting place at the corner of Royal and St. Francis Streets.

Not long after, the Alabama Hotel was built next door to the Franklin, but both buildings were destroyed by fire in 1829. The Waverly Hotel took their place at the same location, but it, too, was destroyed by fire in 1850, after which the original Battle House Hotel was built on that same location.

The Battle House (now called the Battle House Renaissance Mobile Hotel and Spa) was completely rebuilt in 1908 and renovated between 2002 and 2007. Its grand staircase, stained-glass features, intricate plaster moldings and the Crystal Ballroom were completely restored.

The city's infrastructure began to develop, with water pipes being laid to carry fresh water to homes not only within the city but also in rural areas along Springhill Avenue. A successful theater owner, New Orleans' James Caldwell, opened the city's first theater, the Mobile Theater, in 1840. Caldwell illuminated his theaters with natural gas lighting, which he piped to the entire city, and then installed gas streetlights in businesses and homes lining the downtown streets.

At the mouth of Mobile Bay, where the bay meets the Gulf of Mexico, on Dauphin Island to the west and at the tip of a long, sandy peninsula to the east where the former Fort Bowyer once stood, the federal government began constructing two massive stone forts, Fort Morgan and Fort Gaines. The decision to build these two Third System Forts came after the British attempt to take Fort Bowyer during the War of 1812.

Construction of Fort Morgan began in 1819 and Fort Gaines in 1821. Both were built by skilled masons, many of whom were enslaved African Americans. Fort Morgan was a pentagon in shape, which allowed it to protect both the bay and Gulf sides of the peninsula from foreign invaders. The fortress was built with more than 46 million cubic yards of bricks and was completed in 1834.

It was during the antebellum period that Mobile's Creole community played key roles in the development of the city. The Creoles of Mobile were direct descendants of the city's early French and Spanish settlers. In Mobile's early years, many slave owners took enslaved women to bed. It was during the antebellum period that their mixed-race offspring became key members of the community and the development of Mobile. One of their most important contributions concerned the establishment of the city's new volunteer fire department.

Each ward in the city established a volunteer fire department, with the first being the Creole Steam Fire Company No. 1. The city procured its first fire engine, a simple wooden box on wheels that carried empty buckets. The city gave the "engine" to Jean Baptiste Trenier, who used it as the centerpiece to organize Creole Steam Fire Company No. 1 on March 13, 1819. Eighty men joined the brigade, and they were all needed.

Being a firefighter in those days was hard, demanding and dangerous work. The call would go out that there was a fire when the men heard the clanging of a hanging metal rim taken from one of the wheels of the fire wagon that was beaten with a hammer.

The men would pull the cart by hand through the deep, sandy streets of Mobile to the fire, and once there, they would fill the buckets at cisterns. These wells were few and far between, so the men would have to form a bucket brigade—a line of men that would pass the buckets of water one at a time to the actual fire. Every house in the city usually had its own ladder and axes so the fire company didn't need to bring their own. Plus the tallest buildings in town were only two stories tall.

Creole Fire Company No. 1 responded to its first fire in September 1819 when Judson's Cotton Gin on Dauphin Street between Royal and Water Streets went ablaze, and the men made quick work of putting out the fire. The following month, another building, Planters Alley, caught on fire, but

Left: The city's first volunteer fire department, the Creole Steam Fire Company No. 1, became professional paid firefighters, and this station was built for them in 1869. It is now a private home. *Author's collection.*

Below: This restored building on South Claiborne Street was the home of one of Mobile's early fire companies, the Phoenix Volunteer Fire Company No. 6, and today houses Mobile's fire department museum. *Author's collection.*

this time the men were not as successful in their efforts and quickly found themselves surrounded by the flames. They were forced to abandon the engine, which was destroyed. It was replaced with a new engine donated by local resident James Innerarity.

In addition to businesses and hotels, residential housing began to pop up throughout the city. Generally, these houses reflected a Federalist/Classical style. Many of these grand houses have long since been demolished for various reasons. Others that still stand are under private ownership, with limited access by the general public permitted during the Mobile Historic Homes Tour, held annually the first weekend of April (see the "Your Guide to History" section for details).

There are several homes from this era that have been restored and converted into museums that reflect the antebellum period in Mobile. The oldest is the Conde-Charlotte Museum House on Theater Street, directly behind the reproduction of Fort Conde. It is believed that the Conde-Charlotte House actually began as the city's first jail in 1822 before it was renovated by Jonathan and Elizabeth Kirkbride in 1850, becoming his family home.

What makes the Conde-Charlotte House fascinating are the artifacts that have been found on the property and are on display inside. Cell doors and the floor of the jail can still be seen, while many of the rooms have been set up to show what life was like in each of the early periods of Mobile history—French, Spanish, British, Confederate and American.

Another of the homes of the period still with us today and open to the public is the historic Oakleigh House, located in the historic Oakleigh District. Construction on the Greek Revival–style home began in 1833 on thirty-five acres of land purchased with a loan of $20,000 by cotton broker James W. Roper. The grand building represented the quintessential image one would expect from an antebellum home in the South, with a large, sweeping staircase inviting guests inside and bricks hand-made from the clay dug on the property.

Unfortunately for Roper, and much of Mobile, only four years later, a great depression—the Panic of 1837—struck, and Roper was not able to pay off his loan. The house was repossessed, but Roper's brother-in-law, Boyd Simpson, bought back the land and house and allowed Roper and his family to remain there.

The Panic of 1837 was one of several economic collapses that occurred during this period. There were many reasons for the collapse, including inflation that was running out of control and the establishment of new financial institutions, particularly in the South, that were not bound by any regulatory oversight.

One bank, however, was beyond reproach and became known as the "little monster with many heads": the Bank of Mobile. The bank was established in November 1819. The fantastical moniker came from the fact that the bank was one of the few in the entire country that was able to withstand the Panic of 1837 and many other such financial panics.

In 1818, the bank raised $8,750 in gold and silver in order to obtain its charter from the city, but just prior to its opening one year later, the bank was robbed and $3,100 stolen. It was the first bank robbery in the state of Alabama. The culprit, George Bohannan, was eventually caught, but the money was never recovered. He was sentenced to thirty-nine lashes and three hours in the town pillory for the crime.

Education was a priority for the fledgling city during the antebellum period. In 1826, Willoughby Barton began a campaign to create the first public school system in Mobile. The city established a new school commission

Alabama's first public school, Barton Academy, on Government Street. *Author's collection.*

that raised $50,000 for the construction of a new school on Government Street through a lottery, with an additional $15,000 from private funding and a municipal loan.

Famed New Orleans architects James Gallier Sr. and brothers James and Charles Dakin were brought in to design the new school, and in 1839, Barton Academy was completed. Local historian John Sledge best described the Greek Revival architecture of Barton Academy: "A landmark example of Greek Revival style with its columned rotunda floating among the live oak tops, soaring ionic porticoes…and distinguished cast iron fence."

When Barton Academy first opened its doors, it wasn't actually a public school. The builders had amassed great cost overruns and had to repay the debt, so the first students to attend the school had to pay a tuition fee. The school commission also leased out classrooms to private schools. A decade later, the commission reorganized the city's school system, and Barton Academy was reopened this time as a true public school.

Also at this time, the first bishop of Mobile, Michael Portier, envisioned construction of not only the grand Cathedral Basilica of Immaculate Conception but also an institution of higher learning. He purchased three hundred acres of land six miles west of the city, and in 1830, Spring Hill College was opened, the first Catholic college in the Southeast. Today, the college is the third-oldest Jesuit college and the fifth-oldest Catholic college in the country.

The seminary and boarding school sat high atop a hill with a panoramic view of the city and bay. Teachers from France were recruited to educate both high school and college students. The high school eventually closed down in 1935, but the college continues to this day.

Antebellum Mobile saw several famous figures pay a visit. On April 2, 1851, a headline in the *New York Times* announced the arrival of Lajos Kossuth, the man who led Hungary's struggle for independence from Austria. The article said that Kossuth arrived unannounced after visiting New Orleans. Mobile was a whistle-stop for the political reformer, but because there were no boats sailing up the river to Montgomery that night, his stay in the city was "a mere accident."

A committee of businessmen and city commissioners convinced Kossuth to address the city the following day. The *Times* reported that Kossuth obliged and drew a crowd that was "the largest collection ever assembled before in one place in Mobile."

Another foreign dignitary graced the city in 1825: George Washington's former aide, Marquis de Lafayette. The general came to America from

France to support the colonists' revolution and was doing a tour of the United States in celebration of the country's fiftieth anniversary.

A national dignitary made his last appearance ever when he visited Mobile in April 1853. Newspaper accounts from April 12 announced the arrival of the thirteenth vice president of the United States, William Rufus de Vane King, to the port city. King was born in Sampson County, South Carolina, but found a home in Alabama years later when he purchased a cotton plantation near Selma. King studied law and was admitted to the bar in 1806 but quickly made the jump to politics soon after, being elected to the Alabama state legislature and then the U.S. House of Representatives before being elected vice president under President Franklin Pierce.

King was suffering from tuberculosis during the election of 1852. In fact, he was feeling so poorly that he did not attend the inauguration in March of that year. Instead, he and his family sailed to Cuba, where his doctors believed the tropical climate would help his condition. While there, he took the oath of office, being the first and only vice president to be sworn in on foreign soil.

When King arrived in Mobile on that spring day in 1853, he disembarked from the steamer *Junior* at Dog River, just south of the city, and completed his journey to the Government Street wharf in a shallow-draft boat along with his family. An immense crowd had gathered along the waterfront to greet the vice president but were surprised to see his condition. According to the *New York Times*:

> *Colonel King came forward supported by two officers…and was conducted to a carriage provided for the purpose. He appeared to be extremely feeble and attenuated, though he bore his head erect, and his eyes glanced around seemingly with a sad, though pleased interest, to find himself once more on the soil of his beloved Alabama—the Land of Rest.*

King and his entourage made their way to the Battle House Hotel, where they spent the night before returning to his plantation. On April 17, King passed away at his plantation, the third vice president (at the time) to die while in office.

As for socialites who moved to the city during the antebellum area, there was one woman from Augusta, Georgia, who moved to town with her parents in 1835 and quickly became known as the quintessential southern host of the city: Octavia Walton. Soon after arriving in Mobile, Octavia married the highly successful Mobile physician Dr. Henry Strachey Levert and made the decision to use the honorific "Madame" instead of "Mrs.," becoming known as Madame Levert.

Octavia was known for throwing lavish parties and supporting the city's arts and music. She was also a writer, authoring books on her travels to Europe, where she met Queen Victoria. In 1855, Octavia was appointed Alabama's commissioner to the Paris Exhibition, the only woman commissioner at the expo.

Madame Levert had strong convictions about societal norms of the times, finding the role of women to be subservient to their husbands hard to swallow. As the Civil War gripped the nation, Octavia did not approve of secession and was doubtful of the role of slavery in the country. As the story goes, when she received word that General Lee had surrendered to General Grant in Virginia, she ran into the home of Confederate admiral Raphael Semmes on Government Street and cheered the news. She even went as far as to entertain Yankee officers in her home when they arrived in the city in 1865.

Octavia's husband, Dr. Levert, died in 1864. The war had taken its toll on the fortunes of the wealthiest across the South, including Octavia, who was left destitute. Between this and being seen as a traitor for her Yankee sympathizing, Madame Levert left Mobile and returned to Augusta, where she lived out the rest of her storied life.

From the city's earliest days, when Iberville and Bienville established the first settlement on the banks of the Mobile River in 1702, religion has played a significant role in the lives of Mobilians. One year after the establishment of the first fort at Twenty-Seven Mile Bluff, the first Catholic parish on the Gulf Coast was established.

In 1704, Father Henri Roulleaux De la Vente was canonically installed as the first pastor of the Church of Fort Louis de la Louisiane. When the fort was later moved to the present-day location of Mobile in 1711, the church moved with it to a location on the west side of Royal Street just north of Conti Street as Our Lady of Mobile. When Spain took control of Mobile, the church was renamed the Church of the Immaculate Conception.

In 1829, Bishop Michael Portier was made the first bishop of Mobile. He had a vision as to what the future held for the city and wanted to construct a cathedral that would reflect that vision. Soon, he began laying the foundation for that dream: the Cathedral Basilica of Immaculate Conception. The cathedral was completed in December 1850. During the patronal feast, Bishop Martin John Spalding said of the spectacular structure, "It is almost worthy of God."

The beautiful altar in the main sanctuary of the Cathedral Basilica of the Immaculate Conception. *Author's collection.*

Over the years, many of the bishops have added their own touch to the building's history: the iconic tower and steeple was added by the fourth bishop, Jeremiah O'Sullivan; an exquisite gold sanctuary and marble flooring was added by Bishop Thomas J. Toolen; a crypt where the bishops would be buried was added in 1962; and the creation of Cathedral Square in front of the building was overseen by Bishop John L. May.

At the Government Street Presbyterian Church, a Presbyterian congregation was established in 1831 and is recognized as the "Mother of Presbyterianism in Alabama." Its beautiful columned church, located at the corner of Government and South Jackson Streets, has been described as the "state's finest and least-altered example of the Greek Revival style in a religious edifice" by the Society of Architectural Historians. Construction of the church was spearheaded and primarily funded by Alabama's first millionaire, Henry Hitchcock, a Vermont native who moved to Mobile during the city's golden age.

The tombstones of the old Church Street Cemetery, located behind the main branch of the city library on Government Street. *Author's collection.*

As was the case in the town of Blakeley, Mobile was not immune to the effects of the dreaded silent killer yellow fever. Outbreaks of the fever would occur annually throughout the antebellum period, with eleven separate and major epidemics rampaging through the port city between 1819 and 1853. The worst outbreak occurred in August 1819, when more than nine thousand residents died, causing the city to purchase and hastily open a new cemetery: Church Street Cemetery.

As Daryn Glassbrook pointed out in an article found in the July 2021 edition of *Mobile Bay Magazine*, the yellow fever scare gripped the city in fear. Many passengers and crews arriving on train were not allowed to disembark, and if they did, they would have to hold up in quarantine. Cargo on ships and trains were fumigated, and areas within the city were forced into mandatory quarantine.

In 1836, a renowned doctor of the time, Josiah Nott, arrived in Mobile from South Carolina with his family, quickly earning a reputation as an accomplished and competent physician, surgeon and researcher of medical science. Working with Drs. Henry S. Levert (Madame LeVert's husband) and William B. Crawford, Nott was successful in raising the professional medical standards in the city and, in 1841, established the Mobile Medical Society.

The society's focus was on sanitation as a method of overcoming the disease. Meanwhile, those who could afford to moved out of the city and to the then rural areas of Springhill, while others stayed in the city and formed the Can't Get Away Club, providing food and medical assistance to those who were afflicted with the fever.

Nott wrote in a medical journal in 1848 that the disease was coming not from unsanitary conditions or swamp gas but instead mosquitoes, and while his initial writings were dismissed by many in the medical community, it turned out that he was correct; eventually, a vaccine was created to combat the silent killer. Unfortunately, it was too late for Nott's family, who contracted the disease while staying at his father-in-law's house in Springhill. His brother-in-law and four of his children died.

While the yellow fever epidemics of the antebellum period brought the city to its knees, they didn't kill its spirit. That would occur in only a few years as a civil war broke out, pitting brother against brother.

YOUR GUIDE TO HISTORY

Barton Academy
504 Government Street, Mobile
bartonacademy.org
Admission: Free

Despite a long closure and a downward spiral in its care that began in the 1960s, Barton Academy has been completely renovated and is once again a jewel in the Mobile Public School System. Although the building is closed to the public (it is an active school), it is still an impressive and beautiful building to view from the sidewalk on Government Street.

Bragg-Mitchell Mansion
1906 Springhill Avenue, Mobile
(251) 471-6364
braggmitchellmansion.com
Admission: Fee

The thirteen-thousand-square-foot Greek Revival–style Bragg-Mitchell Mansion was built in 1855 by Judge John Bragg for this family to enjoy coastal Alabama living during what was called "Mobile's Social Season"—Thanksgiving through Mardi Gras. The rest of the year, the Braggs lived on their plantation just outside Montgomery. Tours are offered Tuesday through Fridays on the hour beginning at 10:00 a.m., with the last tour at 3:00 p.m.

Cathedral Basilica of the Immaculate Conception
2 South Claiborne Street, Mobile
(251) 434-1565
mobilecathedral.org
Admission: Free

The doors of the cathedral are open to the public. Walk across the beautiful square where many events are held throughout the year, enter the main sanctuary and gaze at the breathtaking stained-glass windows and the impressive marble columns bordering the gleaming altar. Visit its website for times of mass.

The beautiful Cathedral Basilica of the Immaculate Conception. *Author's collection.*

Christ Church Cathedral

115 South Conception Street, Mobile

(251) 438-1822

christchurchcathedralmobile.org

Admission: Free

With its towering columns and amazing Tiffany stained-glass windows, the Christ Church Cathedral is the oldest Presbyterian church in Alabama.

Church of the Good Shepherd

Church Street Cemetery

125 South Scott Street, Mobile (directly behind the Ben May Branch of the Mobile Public Library on Government Street)

cityofmobile.org/parks-rec/cemeteries/church-street-graveyard

Admission: Free

Church Street Cemetery is the oldest surviving cemetery in Mobile. It was established in 1819 as a replacement for the first colonial cemetery, which was located where the Cathedral Basilica of the Immaculate Conception is located. Church Street was established on the outskirts of the city and was initially used to bury victims of a yellow fever epidemic. A walk through the graveyard is highlighted with impressive cast- and wrought-iron ironwork that showcase the artistry of the Victorian period. The cemetery was closed when a new cemetery, Magnolia, was created.

Conde-Charlotte House

104 Theater Street, Mobile
(251) 432-4722
condecharlotte.com
Admission: Fee

This antebellum home turned museum on a side street behind Fort Conde takes visitors back through all phases of Mobile history, with rooms depicting life under French and British rule and, of course, the antebellum period.

Trace Mobile's history back to French rule at the Conde-Charlotte House Museum. *Author's collection.*

Fort Gaines
51 Bienville Boulevard, Dauphin Island
(251) 861-6992
townofdauphinisland.org/things-to-do/historic-fort-gaines
Admission: Fee

See the "Your Guide to History" section in chapter 9.

Fort Morgan Historic Site
110 Highway 180, Gulf Shores
(251) 540-5257
fort-morgan.org
Admission: Fee

See the "Your Guide to History" section in chapter 9.

**Government Street Presbyterian/
Government Street Union Baptist Church**
Historic Blakely State Park
34745 AL 225, Spanish Fort
(251) 626-0798
blakeleypark.com
Admission: Fee

Roam the streets of this 1819 ghost town that once rivaled Mobile as a major cotton exporter. Along the original main street, view the remains of the town of Blakeley's town hall. Blakeley is also the site of the last major battle of the Civil War.

Magnolia Cemetery
1202 Virginia Street, Mobile
(251) 432-8672
magnoliacemetery.com
Admission: Free

Only blocks from downtown Mobile, Magnolia Cemetery was established in 1836 in what was then outside the city limits, replacing the old Church Street Cemetery. At the time, the cemetery was only thirty-six acres, but today it encompasses 120 acres and is the final resting place of many of Mobile's most famous people—the founder of Mardi Gras and the Cowbellion de Rakin Society's Michael Krafft; Dr. Josiah C. Nott, the physician who first reported that mosquitoes transmitted yellow fever; and many more. Walk down the "streets" of this city of the dead and take in the magnificent Victorian-era funerary artistry, each monument and tombstone telling its own story.

Oakleigh House Museum

350 Oakleigh Place, Mobile
(251) 432-1281
historicoakleigh.com
Admission: Fee

Oakleigh is the quintessential mansion of the antebellum period, with tall oaks lining the walkway and a grand staircase inside that leads to room after room of history from this period in Mobile history. Tours of the home built in 1833 are given daily on the hour. The museum is closed Sundays and Mondays.

Old Catholic Cemetery

1700 Martin Luther King Jr. Avenue, Mobile
(251) 479-5305
Admission: Free

Established by the Archdiocese of Mobile in 1848, this 150-acre cemetery is the resting place of Confederate admiral Raphael Semmes and the "Poet Priest of the Confederacy," Father Abram Joseph Ryan.

Richards-DAR House

256 North Joachim Street, Mobile
(251) 208-7320
richardsdarhouse.com
Admission: Fee

Built by Captain Charles G. Richards for his wife, Caroline Elizabeth Steele, in 1860, the Richards DAR House is a gorgeous example of the Italianate style. Inside, visitors are greeted with Carrara marble mantelpieces, the splendor of its cantilevered staircase and room after room of period furnishings. The museum is open Mondays and Fridays through Sundays.

Spring Hill College
4000 Dauphin Street, Mobile
(251) 380-4000
shc.edu
Admission: Free, fee for Spring Hill Badger baseball

The oldest Catholic college in the Southeast and third-oldest Jesuit college in the United States, Spring Hill College was established in 1830 as both a high school and college. Today, much of the campus looks as it did in the 1800s, including Stan Galle Field, which first hosted intercollegiate baseball in Mobile in 1889.

State Street AME Zion Church
502 State Street, Mobile
(251) 432-3965
Admission: Free; visit inside during service

The State Street AME Zion Church is the oldest Methodist church building in Alabama, having been built in the 1820s. It is also one of two African American churches founded in the Methodist religion prior to the Civil War.

Stone Street Baptist Church
311 Tunstall Street, Mobile
(251) 433-3947
stonestreetbc.org
Admission: Free; visit inside during service

The Stone Street congregation first held services in 1806. The building was constructed in 1843 when the white congregation of the St. Anthony Street Baptist Church purchased the land for use by the African American Baptist community. In 1868, the title for the property was transferred to the Stone Street congregation.

Chapter 7

OUT OF SLAVERY

CODE NOIR, THE LAST SLAVE SHIP AND AFRICATOWN

S lavery has always been at the forefront of American history, playing a dynamic role in the rise, fall and rise again of the country's 240-plus-year history. The role of this tragic element of American history takes the fore in the Deep South, and while the Alabama Gulf Coast—Mobile and Baldwin Counties—was less tied to slave labor compared to other parts of the state, where cotton was king and this "cheap" labor force made even the smallest plantation owner a handsome profit, it still played a role in making Mobile at one time the third-largest seaport in the country—and it was all built on the backs of these Black slaves. Two of the most important tales from this piece of history—the story of the last slave ship, the *Clotilda*, and the establishment of Africatown—occur in Mobile, but before we touch on those stories, we need to know how slavery came to be in what would become Mobile.

Throughout the history of slavery, European countries believed that Africa and the inhabitants of the West Indies were uncivilized and "heathens," so they believed that using these people as slave labor, stripping them of their rights and freedoms to do the backbreaking work required to build new settlements, was actually giving them a better life. Of course, that view was tinged with racism and the immoral attitude that these people could be simply sold and treated as property.

As early as 1701, when brothers Jean Baptiste Le Moyne, Sieur de Bienville, and Pierre Le Moyne d'Iberville were colonizing the North

American Gulf Coast, it became quite evident to the men that they would need an expanded workforce to help cultivate the land and help the new settlements prosper. The land near the bay and in the delta were ripe for cultivation. The soil was fertile from the yearly flooding and the myriad rivers and streams that fed the delta and eventually created the bay that flowed into the Gulf. As botanist to the queen of England, William Bartram wrote years later that the bay showed great promise for the profitable growth of tobacco, corn, potatoes, beans, peas, pears, grapes and plums. The problem for the early French colonies, as we learned previously, was that the settlers Bienville and d'Iberville brought to Mobile were not inclined to perform any agricultural duties.

Bienville wrote to the lieutenant governor of the Louisiana territory, asking for the transportation of slaves from Caribbean islands to work the soil. His request was ignored. He wrote again in 1707 and still received no response. In 1708, Bienville requested that the colonists be allowed to send Native Americans to the islands of the West Indies in exchange for Black slaves from the islands. The request was denied. The early Mobile colonists went on to rely on Native American slave labor to till the soil.

By 1716, there were only a few Black people located in and around the Mobile area, but that would change in 1717, when the West India Company was given control of all commerce for French Louisiana. The company stated that it was dedicated to the agricultural development of the territory and felt "obliged" to transport Black laborers to the region for the purpose of achieving this mission.

In March 1721, the first slave trade ship, the *Africane*, arrived in Mobile. The ship left Guinea with 240 captured Black men, women and children, but only 120 survived the voyage. The *Africane* arrived in port at a most inopportune moment. The settlement at Mobile was facing a severe food shortage, and famine was running rampant. Many of the enslaved who disembarked the ship came close to starvation while being housed in the settlement.

From that moment, slave ships arrived yearly. Two other ships arrived in Mobile in 1721: the *Marie*, which embarked on its voyage from Africa with 338 captives, and the *Neride*, which set sail from Angola with 350 captives, of which 112 died en route. In fact, many of those who were captured and sent by ship to the new settlement died of dysentery, scurvy or measles.

The conditions for enslaved Black men, women and children through to the Civil War was deplorable to say the least, being given ragged clothes to wear, living in single- or two-room shacks with a hearth for cooking and dirt

Mobile artist and director of the Federal Museum Richbourg Gailiard demonstrates a bell and rack in 1937. The device was used by Alabama slave owners to guard a runaway slave. The rack was originally topped by a bell, which rang when the runaway attempted to leave the road and go through foliage or trees. It was attached around the neck, as shown in the picture. A belt passed through the loop at the bottom to hold the iron rod firmly fastened to the waist of the wearer. *Library of Congress, Prints and Photographs Division, Washington, D.C., 20540 USA.*

floors; the combination of unsanitary conditions and inadequate nutrition resulted in many deaths.

Both men and women shared the brunt of the work on farms—clearing and tilling the land, cultivating and harvesting the crops, raising cattle and constructing and maintaining buildings. Some of the men were able to learn trades and worked in urban, industrial areas, like Mobile, where they worked the cotton gins and became blacksmiths, bakers and shoemakers.

Women also helped with the backbreaking work of tending to the farm and acted as midwives, assisting their white owners with child-rearing. Given the lack of white women, many slave owners took enslaved women to their beds. This gave rise to one of the oldest communities of people of color in the city, the direct descendants of Mobile's early French and Spanish settlers and either free or slave African Americans, the Creole community.

Enslaved people had limited, if any, rights. They were allowed to go to church and sometimes allowed to take holidays off. But in the early years of colonization, slaves could be harshly punished for misbehavior with lashes by the whip or pinching with red hot iron tongs for stealing or trying to escape. That punishment was later reduced to a more "humane" treatment where the slave could be whipped or shackled but not maimed.

By the time the West India Company's contract expired, it had transported more than seven thousand enslaved Black people to the French Louisiana territory. Once in Mobile, the captured Black people were sold to the ever-growing number of plantations around Mobile Bay, but only to those plantation owners who could offer food, clothing and housing for the slaves and who could afford the cost. Slaves were sold for $176, payable by three yearly installments.

The Code Noir, or Black Code, was introduced to French Louisiana in 1724. The Code was a set of rules governing the practice of slavery and, in particular, defining the legal status of enslaved Black people. The Code set out to define the conditions of slavery—that is, the status of a captured person. For example, if any free man had sexual relations with an enslaved woman, the man and the slave owner would be fined. If a slave owner and female slave had relations and she bore a child, the child would be taken from the mother and given to a hospital as a slave. If a free man married an enslaved woman in a church, the woman would become free, as would her children. In general, with the birth of a child, the child would have the status of the mother—if she were enslaved, the children would be as well; if she were free, the children would be free.

The last sale from the slave trade during Mobile's French period came in 1759, when three French frigates carrying 414 slaves were seized by a British vessel. Four years later, the Louisiana Superior Council passed a law forbidding any further transportation of Black people from certain locations because so many whites were being poisoned by the location's Black population.

It is notable that as the new country was taking shape in 1787, the delegates to the Constitutional Convention debated the issue of slavery fiercely and finally agreed that the importing of slaves from Africa and the West Indies should end within twenty years. In 1800, the *Act Prohibiting the Importation of Slaves* was passed by Congress, and it took effect in 1808.

Most people believe that all enslaved people were imported by ship to southern shores, but in reality, the 1808 law made it quite difficult and almost impossible for that to happen; the majority of slaves were actually moved to the South from northern states as whites flooded the region during the cotton boom.

By the mid-1800s, cotton was king as plantations in the northern and central regions of the state were prospering, and in Mobile, the cotton gins and warehouses were bustling with activity; the accelerated exportation of cotton at the wharf meant there was a need for more workers. White slave owners found the supply of their valued labor force being squeezed off by the law, and the price for enslaved people skyrocketed.

An article in the *New York Times* dated November 17, 1862, summarized how successful the law was, with one notable exception:

> We have the names of over one hundred and fifty vessels which were engaged in the trade from 1858 to 1861.…Of this number, thirty eight were seized on the coast of Africa…and over thirteen thousand negroes were returned to Africa. A correspondent high in official standing writing from Havana stated the fact that upward of 30,000 Africans had been landed on the island during the single year previous.

The article then went on to list the names of the ships and captains who were seized or turned back by British or U.S. vessels. The list went on and on until it came to July 10, 1860, with an entry of note: "The schooner Clotilda landed a cargo of negroes at Mobile. No arrests were made."

The *Clotilda* went down in history as the last slave ship to voyage into the United States, and it landed in Mobile Bay in the summer of 1860, fifty-two years after the prohibition law went into effect. But how could that be?

With the demand for slave labor skyrocketing across the southern cotton states but no way to import more into the country, plantation owner Timothy Meaher made a bet that he could bring a ship load of Africans back to Mobile without being caught by the law.

In early 1860, the *Clotilda*, under command of Captain William Foster, set sail from Mobile and arrived at the Kingdom of Dahomey (now known as the People's Republic of Benin), where he took onboard 110 slaves who had been captured by warring tribes of the region.

Federal authorities did catch word of Meaher's scheme and were keeping watch out for the ship to return, but on July 9, 1860, under the cloak of darkness, the *Clotilda* sailed back into the bay and slipped past federal law enforcement. Captain Foster transferred the captives to a riverboat and sent it north into the backwaters of the delta, where the captured Africans disembarked into the swamps. Meanwhile, the ship was set afire and sunk to hide the evidence.

Soon, the captives were split up between the captain and Meaher, with the remaining slaves sold to area plantations. In 1861, the federal government finally brought Meaher to trial to face charges of violating the prohibition, but the case was dismissed either because of the lack of evidence or because the Civil War had begun.

Five years later, after the *Clotilda* arrived in Mobile and following the Civil War, the *Clotilda* slaves were freed by Union soldiers. Not having enough money to return to Africa, thirty-two of the former slaves pooled the money they had earned from growing vegetables and working fields to purchase land from the Meaher family, the same family who brought them to the United States. On that land, they created their own community: Africatown.

Africatown is unique in that it's a community that was completely built by former slaves and was self-governing. One of the last surviving members of the slaves who founded Africatown, Oluale Kossla, better known as Cudjo Lewis, passed away in 1934, but before his passing, Lewis left behind a detailed record of his life and the founding of Africatown in a fascinating book, *Barracoon*, in which Lewis laid bare the *Clotilda* story to author Zora Neale Hurston.

In 2019, the charred remains of the *Clotilda* were discovered and verified in the sediment of the delta. Discussions are currently underway on how best to preserve this incredible piece of history.

The story of the *Clotilda* and Africatown is an intricate web of events that deserves more attention than I can give here. I highly recommend that you

Cudjo Lewis pictured with another survivor of the last slave ship, *Abache*, around 1830. *"Abache and Kazoola," Mobile Public Library Digital Collections, http://digital. mobilepubliclibrary.org/ items/show/1830.*

read *Barracoon* and also the highly acclaimed book by Ben Raines *The Last Slave Ship* to continue the story.

As the Civil War approached, the city had the largest population of free people of color in the state. The 1860 census reported that eight hundred free Blacks lived in the city, plus more than one thousand slaves lived inside the city limits apart from their masters. Many of these freed men and women owned and operated their own businesses, especially barbershops. In fact, more than half of the barbershops in Mobile were operated by free men of color. This caused much concern for the whites of the community, who were under the misguided impression that these businesses, as well as the city's Black churches, were havens for discussions of insurrection and revolts by slaves. They believed that these meeting places were where the free Blacks would discuss ways to cause a slave revolt against their owners.

The state proposed several options to attempt to quell a slave revolt, which never occurred or was actually actively pursued. The state legislature proposed laws that would require free Blacks to either leave the state altogether—preferably back to their country of origin—or be rounded up and sold into servitude by the state.

Strict laws were handed down that made life increasingly difficult for freemen. The city levied excessive taxes on free Blacks, even instituting curfews that were meant to keep them off the streets at night unless a special pass was granted by the mayor.

The free people of color throughout the city felt as if they were trapped: they had a reasonable amount of freedom, but now that freedom and their way of life, even their lives themselves, were being threatened. Many believed that to be protected from the harassment and violence that was unfolding, their best option was to relinquish their freedom and become slaves themselves. The state went on to establish a regulation whereby free people of color could submit petitions to the Mobile probate office to do just that: go from a free status to slave.

To qualify, the regulation stipulated that a new "master" had to be identified, both the "master to be" and the free Black person would be required to declare their intentions and declare that the petition was being submitted on the free man's own free will. After that, a hearing on the matter would take place within ten days of the petition being filed.

The future master was not allowed to acquire the new slave and then turn around and sell him or her to someone else to pay off debts and had to pay the filing fee of five dollars; additionally, if the person petitioning the court was under eighteen, they would have to pay a fifteen-dollar fee for the service of an attorney who would be assigned to the case.

Many of these petitions can be viewed on microfiche today in the Mobile Local History and Genealogy Library on Government Street. The petitions paint a sad tale of the fear that was gripping these people. In one case, a young woman requested the change of status due to the fact that her husband had passed away, and since that time, she had been working as a servant for a wealthy doctor. She was on her own with no family and no income. In the petition, she states that after "mature deliberation on her part" and "uninfluenced by any person," she felt that her condition in life would be better because she was presently "destitute and without protection"; as a slave, she would be cared for and protected, to some degree. Many of the petitions are simply signed with an "X" due to the fact that many could not write.

On April 9, 1865, the Civil War ended, and the formal institution of slavery was soon abolished in the country. But over the next few decades, an era of racial disparity, segregation and terror would take its place that would eventually lead to long-overdue national civil rights laws and bring the country's creed that "all men are created equal" one step closer to reality.

YOUR GUIDE TO HISTORY

Black Education Museum
1000 Main Street, Daphne
(251) 510-0355
daphneal.com/276/Arts-Museums
Admission: Free

Clotilda
Historic Blakeley State Park, 34745 AL 225, Spanish Fort
(251) 626-0798
blakeleypark.com/cruises
Admission: Fee for park admission and cruise

The remains of the last slave ship, the *Clotilda*, can be seen on special cruises conducted by Delta Explorer out of Historic Blakeley State Park.

Dora Franklin Finley African American Heritage Trail
111 South Royal Street, Mobile
(251) 725-2236
dffaaht.org
Admission: Donation requested

The best way to explore Mobile's African American history is to take one of the tours offered by the Dora Franklin Finley African American Heritage Trail. The trail's board of directors sums up the tour perfectly: develop a taste for the rich gumbo of ethnicity of Mobile's past and enhance your lifelong understanding of the African American's role in Mobile history. Several tours are offered that encompass the whole of this history, with visits to Africatown, Big Zion AME, Creole Fire House No. 1, Unity Point, Dr. H. Roger Williams Drug Store and many more.

Driving Tour of African American History
Start at 735 South Washington Avenue, Mobile
theclio.com/tour/1612
Admission: Free except for admission to the History Museum of Mobile and the Mobile Carnival Museum

Take this self-driving tour to sixteen sites of historical significance regarding the history of African Americans in Mobile, including the Mobile Carnival Museum; the Bettie Hunter House, built by a businesswoman and former slave; Stone Street Baptist Church; and more.

National African American Archives and Multicultural Museum

564 Dr. Martin Luther King Jr. Avenue, Mobile
(251) 433-8511
facebook.com/people/National-African-American-Archives-Multicultural-Museum/100057603963449
Admission: Fee

The museum houses an extensive oral history collection chronicling African American history in Mobile and is dedicated to the preservation of this history. Within the archives and museum, you will find portraits, biographies, African carvings, an extensive collection of books, family histories, antique artifacts and other memorabilia.

Old Plateau Africatown Cemetery

1954 Old Bay Bridge Road, Mobile
Admission: Free

Pay your respects to the survivors of the *Clotilda* and the African American families who founded Africatown at the Old Plateau Africatown Cemetery. A project is continuing to identify the three thousand graves believed to be present in the cemetery. There is a tall marker for Cudjo Lewis, who is buried in the cemetery.

Chapter 8

BORN TO CELEBRATE

THE BIRTH OF MARDI GRAS

From San Diego to New York City and points in between, the United States loves to celebrate Mardi Gras, the one time of the year when people can let their inhibitions melt away before the season of Lent. Of course, we are all familiar with the largest and rowdiest Mardi Gras (also called Carnival) celebration in the country. That would be in New Orleans, so most people naturally associate the Crescent City as being the birthplace of the party. In reality, the first city (or settlement, really) to celebrate the holiday was Mobile more than three hundred years ago, which comes as a huge surprise to most people. As we will see, while Mobile had the first recorded celebration, Mobile and New Orleans, two of the first French settlements on the Gulf Coast, have traded Mardi Gras traditions back and forth over the years, such traditions as the first street parades, the formation of mystic societies and the concept of Mardi Gras balls. All of these traditions built on one another, merging into the celebrations we all know today.

Mardi Gras is believed to have started thousands of years ago during the Roman empire as a pagan celebration of the arrival of spring and fertility. As Christianity spread throughout Europe during medieval times, the church decided—as it did with many pagan celebrations—to incorporate Roman celebrations into the religious calendar and made the festival the prelude to Lent. The actual celebration would fall on the Tuesday before Lent, which is the period of forty days between Ash Wednesday and Easter Sunday and is a time of prayer, fasting and alms giving. It was the French who would give the celebration a name—Mardi Gras, which means Fat Tuesday.

Before we look at the history of Mardi Gras in Mobile and America, there needs to be a little clarification for those who are not familiar with the holiday. It can be a little confusing.

As mentioned, Mardi Gras is a single day, Fat Tuesday, but the two names are interchangeable. It is a single day when people let down their hair and throw their inhibitions to the wind. The idea is to let it all out and celebrate like there was no tomorrow with a bit of indulgent eating, drinking and a little promiscuity thrown in before the holy season of Lent begins, when revelers are expected to sacrifice something for their sins.

While Fat Tuesday is still held the day before Ash Wednesday, celebrations around the country have expanded to the two weeks (sometimes even a month) before Mardi Gras itself. The weeks before actual Mardi Gras are called Carnival, but most people refer to the entire parading season as Mardi Gras. Confusing, right? Whatever you call it, Mardi Gras has changed significantly since the first celebration occurred on the shores of Mobile Bay.

The first recorded celebration of Mardi Gras in the New World came on March 2, 1699, courtesy of the founders of Mobile, brothers Jean Baptiste Le Moyne, Sieur de Bienville, and Pierre Le Moyne d'Iberville. In his journal, Bienville made a simple entry, noting that it was Mardi Gras Day. Nothing was written about what the celebration entailed. It certainly was nothing near what we have come to expect today.

The second reference to Mardi Gras once again came from Bienville in 1703, one year after establishing Fort Louis de la Louisiane (which would later become Mobile), but again, there are no records of what that celebration consisted of. The one thing we are sure of is that the first recorded evidence of Mardi Gras being celebrated in North America was in 1703 in Mobile.

The first actual Mardi Gras parade was held in 1711 in Mobile as the townspeople celebrated *Boeuf Gras* (another name for Mardi Gras) with a raucous celebration of food, song and dancing that was highlighted with a papier-mâché bull being pulled down Dauphin Street.

It wasn't until 1830 that a new but key element of Mardi Gras was born: the mystic society. A mystic society is just that—a group of like-minded individuals that form an organization based on economic status, race or sex. Most societies operate in absolute secrecy, wearing masks and costumes to protect their identity. Many modern-day societies recruit members from the general public and outside their circle, but the waiting list to become a member is long.

The societies (known generally as "mystics" in Mobile and "krewes" in New Orleans) are responsible for building the elaborate floats that parade

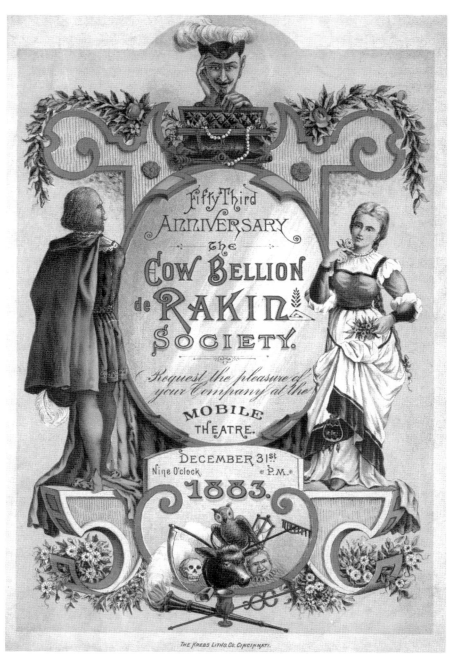

An invitation to a gala ball hosted by Mobile's first Mardi Gras Mystic Society, the Cowbellion de Rakin Society in 1883. *"Cowbellion de Rakin Society 1883," Mobile Public Library Digital Collections, http://digital.mobilepubliclibrary.org/items/show/1734.*

down city streets, with masked revelers from the society riding atop them rocking back and forth to the rhythm of marching bands as they toss goodies such as candy and the coveted beads (better known, appropriately enough, as "throws") to the throngs of onlookers.

The first society was formed by inebriated accident on New Year's Eve 1830. It all began when a man by the name of Michael Kraft and a like-minded group of friends were out celebrating and were in what could be called "jolly spirits." As they walked the streets of Mobile, they passed a hardware store that was located somewhere along the waterfront at the end of Government Street, where the current-day Convention Center and Cooper Riverside Park is located.

Depending on who you talk to, the story deviates a bit. Some say that there were tools on display of rakes and cowbells outside the store, while others say that Kraft sat down on the stoop in front of the store and knocked over a stack of rakes and cowbells. Either way, the group picked up the tools and began parading around town, making quite a racket with the cowbells and holding their rakes up high.

Somewhere along the line, a person stopped them, either a passerby or the actual mayor of Mobile, depending on who is telling the story, and asked them if the group had a name, to which the quick-thinking Kraft replied, "The Cowbellion de Rakin Society!"

Around 1856, six members of the Cowbellions moved to New Orleans and started the Order of Comus, the oldest parading organization in the Crescent City that still hits the streets to this day. The Cowbellions were in existence until the 1890s, when they disbanded, but a few of the societies they inspired are still in existence today, including the Order of Myths, which was established in 1867, and the Infant Mystics, which was organized in 1868.

The Order of Myths was formed while Union troops were still occupying Mobile following the Civil War. The society's name was inspired by the International Order of Odd Fellows (IOOF). Its emblem was designed by Morton Toulmin and had much symbolism. In the center, there is a broken column—the "column of life." Some speculate that this choice was symbolic of the broken spirit of the South after being defeated in the war.

Two figures dance around the column. One is a skeleton with a big, bulky skull that represents Death. The other is the gaily costumed figure of Folly, which represents good times and frivolity. Folly is chasing Death around the column, and as he does so, he is beating Death with an inflated pig's bladder, signifying that on Mardi Gras, Folly defeats Death.

The original floats for the Order of Myths parade in 1868 were mule-drawn carts that were illuminated by people walking alongside them carrying the soft glow of lighted torches or flambeaux. Atop the float was a full-size replica of the column, around which two members of the society dressed as Folly and Death, chased each other. To this day, the Order of Myths is the last parade of Carnival season, using a faithfully re-created mule-drawn cart signifying its end.

Besides the annual parades, the mystic societies organize different events throughout the year for their members, but of course, their big time to shine is during Carnival season. Following the parade, the organizations cap off the evening with an elaborate invitation-only formal ball.

The two main societies that "rule the city" during Carnival are the Mobile Area Mardi Gras Association (MAMGA) and the Mobile Area Carnival Association (MACA). MAMGA is generally an African American organization, while the MACA is of European descent. Each organization chooses a king, who selects a queen, and both are crowned during a special ceremony.

Both the king and queen wear brilliantly bedecked jeweled crowns and costumes that harken back to French royalty. The queen wears a long, flowing train that is generally eighteen feet long and nine feet wide and can weigh more than forty pounds. The train is made of furs, velvet and satin material, all bedazzled with hundreds of glimmering rhinestones, pearls and sequins. Following the coronation, the royal couple preside over various festivities and the society's parade itself.

The first mystic organization royal court was introduced into the celebration in 1872, when Daniel E. Huger was crowned the first King of Carnival as Emperor Felix I. It is believed that Mobile's African American community organized its first society in 1894 with the establishment of the Order of Doves.

During the Civil War and in the subsequent Reconstruction years, Mardi Gras was canceled and didn't return until 1868, when former Confederate soldiers who hailed from Mobile returned and wanted to have some fun. On Fat Tuesday that year, the Order of Myths returned to the streets, as did another group, the Lost Cause Minstrels, a name that was symbolic of the defeated South. The Minstrels were led by Joseph Stillwell "Joe" Cain. Joe Cain, dressed in a fanciful Indian costume, named himself Chief Slacabamorinico, and the first Joe Cain Parade was held.

The Joe Cain Parade still rolls each year the Sunday before Fat Tuesday. Also known as the People's Parade, the parade is for everyday people. There is no royalty or fancy balls, but there is plenty of partying. The parade is led

It looks as if Death is taking a break from being chased by Folly in this 1906 invitation to an Order of Myths ball. *"Order of Myths 1906," Mobile Public Library Digital Collections, http://digital.mobilepubliclibrary. org/items/show/50.*

by a group of revelers dressed in black mourning dresses and veils covering their faces. They are known as Joe Cain's Widows. The "ladies" lead the parade to the Church Street Cemetery, where Cain is buried.

By 1875, Mardi Gras had taken on a life of its own and was a solid tradition in the Port City, so much so that the Alabama state legislature declared Shrove Tuesday (yet another name for Fat Tuesday) as a holiday in the city and encouraged businesses to shut down so that the public could mask up and party.

Besides the party atmosphere along downtown streets, thousands clamor for the best seats along the parade routes so they can shout, "Throw something to me, mister!" and, with luck, catch a coveted throw. The tradition of throwing trinkets to the revelers dates back to Roman times, when ancient Romans would hand out goat hide whips to the crowds at the end of Lupercalia. After the Order of Comus was organized in New Orleans, women en route to Mardi Gras balls would toss candy, bon bons and provocative smiles to men who lined their route. A painting from 1871 for the New Orleans Twelfth

The Mardi Gras tradition continues down the streets of Mobile. *George F. Landegger Collection of Alabama Photographs, Carol M. Highsmith's America, Library of Congress, Prints and Photographs Division.*

Night Revelers shows the final float in the parade carrying Santa Claus, who was tossing candy to the crowd from a bag.

The tradition quickly came to Mobile and has been part of the celebration ever since. The tradition of throwing strands of fake jewels or beads to "loyal subjects" began somewhere in the 1890s, and today, you will see dozens of strands of these plastic beauties dangling from the rearview mirrors of automobiles during the celebration and the limbs of the old oak trees that line the parade routes almost as if they grow on the trees.

In Mobile, the tradition of throwing candy got a new and uniquely Mobile twist in the early 1960s. Up until that point, it was common for revelers to throw boxes of Cracker Jack to the crowd from the floats. As you can imagine, that could be a painful experience if you're bonked on the head with a box.

As the story goes, a group of women from a Mobile mystic society were in Chattanooga, Tennessee, and were treated to a soft chocolate and marshmallow treat: the Moon Pie. The ladies thought that they would make a great replacement for Cracker Jack, and the tradition of tossing Moon Pies to the crowd was born.

Today, next to catching a fistful of beads, the Moon Pie is the most coveted Mardi Gras throw for spectators. The Moon Pie is so revered in Mobile that every year on New Year's Eve, those who come downtown to ring in the new year can eat a slice taken from the world's largest Moon Pie and, at the stroke of midnight, watch a six-hundred-pound electric replica of the treat drop from the RSA Trustmark Tower.

YOUR GUIDE TO HISTORY

Church Street Cemetery

125 South Scott Street, Mobile, AL 36602
cityofmobile.org/parks-rec/cemeteries/church-street-graveyard
Admission: Free
Hours: Year-round, sunrise to sunset

The second-oldest cemetery in Mobile, Church Street, was established in 1819. In terms of Mardi Gras, the cemetery is famous for two grave sites. The first is that of Joe Cain himself. The second is the final resting place of Julian Rayford, who worked to have Cain's remains exhumed and moved to the cemetery from the town of Bayou la Batre so that his contribution to Mardi Gras could be better appreciated. He is also the man who organized the first People's Parade. When you visit, pay your respects by placing beads or doubloons on their graves.

Mardi Gras Park

111 South Royal Street, Mobile
mobile.org/listing/mardi-gras-park/1673
Admission: Free

A statue of Joe Cain as Chief Slac stands guard over the Mardi Gras Tree at Mobile's Mardi Gras Park. *Author's collection.*

Mobile's Mardi Gras Park is located on the site of the old city hall and pays homage to the first Mardi Gras in America. It's also a great vantage point to watch a parade from. The park is rimmed with colorful statues depicting elements of the celebration—the bands, the kings and the queens, Folly and Joe Cain dressed as Chief Slac. During Mardi Gras season, a towering Mardi Gras Tree lights up the square.

Two oversize sculptures of Folly from the Order of Myths society greet you at the entrance to the Mobile Carnival Museum. *Author's collection.*

Mobile Carnival Museum

355 Government Street, Mobile, AL 36602
(251) 432-3324
mobilecarnivalmuseum.com
Admission: $8 adults, $3 children twelve and under, $6 military/students/AARP

More than three hundred years of Mardi Gras history is on display at the Carnival Museum on Government Street. Visitors are welcomed by two grinning statues of Folly as you enter. Inside, see firsthand the history and majesty of the celebration with artifacts from years gone by, including ninety beautiful trains from past Mardi Gras queens.

Chapter 9

DAMN THE TORPEDOES!

As Southern states began dropping like dominoes, peeling away one by one from the "Great Experiment" known as the United States of America, there was talk that maybe, just maybe, Alabama—Mobile in particular—might not secede from the Union. An observer wrote in the *New York Times* on November 20, 1860:

> *A Northerner…recognizing the authority of business interest, will not perhaps be able to understand the motives which could influence thoughtful men for all are not fire-eaters here—whose interests of property are all interwoven with those of the North….The action of Alabama is yet quite questionable, the central or cotton region portion will favor secession, the Northern or grain raising section, and the extreme South (both populous)* [Mobile and Baldwin Counties], *will probably oppose it.*

One month later, on Christmas Day, the *Times* reported that Mobile was actually putting together a group to head to the state's capital, Montgomery, for a convention that would be held in January to discuss secession and to argue against it, or at least have the state take its time before making a hasty decision:

> *On December 17th, a meeting was held in Mobile, Ala., to nominate candidates in opposition to those put forward by the immediate secessionists….Hon. Jeremiah Clemens…expresses himself as favorable to*

the most determined resistance but he sees no reason for undue haste....Mr.
Clemens avows himself a Union man, but favors a final settlement of the
vexed question of Slavery.

Mobile was unique in Alabama. Being the state's only port city and the nation's second-largest port from which cotton was exported, it is understandable why there was some trepidation in some of its citizens about splitting from the Union. It was understood that, upon secession, Mobile Bay would be blockaded by the Union navy, hindering the Port City's ability to ship cotton and other goods. Businesses could be ruined, and Mobile's economy could be destroyed.

But secessionists outnumbered the pro-Union movement, and the state inched ever closer to the inevitable. Upon hearing the news of South Carolina's secession, the city rejoiced. It was reported that the news was "celebrated with the firing of a hundred guns, cheers of people, and a military parade....The bells are ringing merrily and the people are in the streets by the hundreds testifying their joy at the triumphant secession."

Rumors and conspiracy theories began to fill the streets of Mobile that the Civil War was already well underway and that Northern cities, New York in particular, were already in flames, set afire by the Confederacy. From a dispatch to the *New York Times*:

> *Alabama in the "highest state of excitement" and the "most absurd rumors*
> *are afloat, and gain credence. Only two days since the whole city was a stir*
> *with information that New York City was in a state of civil war* [and]
> *that the Times and Tribune buildings had been Burned.*

Even before Alabama had left the Union, the Confederate army and navy were already making moves. On January 3, 1861, it was reported that Fort Morgan had been taken without incident by the Confederates. At 3:00 a.m., four Confederate companies under the command of Colonel John B. Todd set sail from Mobile on the steamer *Kate Dale* and headed south toward the Gulf and the two stone fortresses: Fort Gaines and Fort Morgan. A cadet sent a letter that was reprinted in the *New York Times* the following day about the capture of Fort Morgan:

> *Landed safe last night and arrived without any disturbance. Took charge*
> *of Fort Morgan about 5 o'clock this morning. Men busy clearing up and*
> *fixing for cooking…The Alabama and regimental colors were run up this*

morning at morning gun amidst cheers from the garrison.…The fort is not in as bad repair as we expected to find it.

Alabama's split from the Union was made official on January 11, 1816, when a state convention passed an ordinance that didn't mince words:

An ordinance to dissolve the Union between the State of Alabama and other states united under the compact and style of the United States of America. Whereas the election of Abraham Lincoln and Hannibal Hamlin to the offices of President and Vice President of the United States of America by a sectional party, avowedly hostile to the domestic institutions and peace and security of the people of the state of Alabama, following upon the heels of many and dangerous infractions of the Constitution of the United States…is a political wrong of so insulting and menacing as a character as to justify the people of the State of Alabama in the adoption of prompt and decided measures for their future peace and security. Therefore, be it declared and ordained, by the people of the State of Alabama…that the State of Alabama now withdraws from the Union.

From the outset of the war, the South's financial situation was its biggest failing. The South's economy was tied to land and agriculture, particularly cotton. It was dependent on sales of this commodity to the Northern states and Europe. With a blockade of the Confederacy's ports, of which Mobile and New Orleans were the two largest on the Gulf Coast, and the abandonment of farms, the South's economic situation was on the brink of collapse from the beginning.

As men went to war, farmland went fallow. All men ages eighteen to thirty-five were required to serve three years in the Confederate military. If these men had the means, they could get around the law by paying a substitute to take their place. Most of the men who could buy their way out of the war were rich plantation owners. The practice of paying for a substitute became so rampant that by September 1862, an exemption was added to the law that exclude planters and overseers who supervised twenty or more slaves from serving. A great deal for the wealthy—not so great for the small family farms across the state that were decimated as more and more men marched off to war. Production of cotton was drastically reduced. For every fifteen bales of cotton that was grown in 1861 and 1862, only one was grown in 1864 and 1865.

It wasn't only the abandonment of farms that aided in the South's financial woes. On top of the collapse of agriculture, add in the effect of those engaging in profiteering and those who were stockpiling goods and you have a recipe for disaster.

Continued funding of the war was a challenge for the Confederacy, so much so that the city's newspaper, the *Mobile Register*, published a plea to the city's woman of social power to do the unthinkable and help with the cause:

> *In Mobile, and no doubt in many Southern cities, another expedient is resorted to for the replenishment of the exhausted treasury. The* Mobile Register *calls upon all the married women and widows, and maidens and little girls, to step forward for the relief of the Government. It appeals to them to give up their little pin money, their diamonds, their earrings, their finger-rings, and all other personal ornaments they have to be turned into money for the carrying on of the war.*

Inflation began to take its toll on the population, skyrocketing an incredible 750 percent. A barrel of flour, for example, went from $44 a barrel to $400.

As predicted, upon Alabama's secession from the Union, Mobile Bay was blockaded by the Union navy. It only took a few months for the blockade to start putting even more pressure on the Port City. Food and clothing shortages quickly spread. Residents learned how to deal with little or nothing and concocted ways to make do with whatever they had in the pantry. It even got to the point that there was coffee rationing, but inventive Mobilians produced an alternative: mix a pot of water with a pint of toasted corn meal and boil. It got to the point that the city ran out of oil for streetlamps and had to resort to refilling them with pitch and hard pine knots.

By 1863, the food situation was becoming dire in cities across the South. Mobile had been relying on growers in Mississippi for supplies of corn, but the commander of Confederate troops in that state, Colonel John Pemberton, prohibited its export, citing the need to conserve the corn crops for his own troops and the citizens of his state.

By fall, Mobile mayor R.H. Slough had written a letter that appeared in the *Mobile Register* that was directed at the richest in the city to do their part to help the less fortunate:

> *There are many indigent women especially who need succor. Their own wants and those of their children are calculated to touch the hardest and*

least sympathetic heart. Let us then, my fellow citizens, see that these worthy objects of charity are placed above the reach of absolute destitution. Money for the purpose left at my office, or at that of Capt. D. Wheeler, will be devoted to the purpose with care, so that it may reach the necessities of the most deserving.

By September 4, the women of Mobile had had enough. It was becoming impossible to feed their hungry children, and the situation finally came to a head. Women throughout Mobile met on Spring Hill Road (now Spring Hill Avenue) with every intention of marching on city hall to demand that the city government act on their behalf or they would take matters into their own hands.

A reporter from the *New Orleans Era* newspaper described the throng of women as a "most formidable riot by a long-suffering and desperate population." Some women carried signs that read, "Bread or Blood," while others brandished hatchets, bricks and axes. It was obvious that the women had every intention of breaking into and raiding the stores that lined Dauphin Street.

A drawing depicting Southern women cheering their men on to rebellion and then feeling the effects of rebellion in the form of bread riots. *Library of Congress.*

In an attempt to head off the mob, the Seventh Alabama Regiment of the Confederate army was dispatched with orders to put down the riot by any means necessary. One soldier was quoted as saying, "If we took any action, [we would] rather assist those starving wives, mothers, sisters and daughters of men who had been forced to fight the battles of the rebellion."

With the regiment refusing to obey orders, the Mobile Cadets, a parade and show regiment, was ordered into action and to use force to stop the women if necessary. The reporter from the *New Orleans Era* recalled the event as "quite a little scrimmage [which resulted] in the repulse of the gallant fellows." The women defeated the cadets.

When troops couldn't squelch the riot, the mayor tried negotiating with the women, promising them that if they would disperse, the city would meet their needs. Satisfied with the response, the women headed home, but after thinking it over, they believed that they had been duped and returned later that evening with more anger than before. They raided downtown stores, emptying racks and shelves of clothing, food and household goods.

A *New Orleans Era* reporter told the story of how the Mobile police aided the women:

> *In coming down Dauphine-Street [sic], two women went into a Jew clothing store, in the performance of the work connected with their mission. The proprietor of the store forcibly ejected the intruders, and threw them violently down on the sidewalk. A policeman who happened to be near, thereupon set upon the Jew and gave him a severe beating.*

The women of Mobile vowed that they would burn down the city if their needs weren't met. The riot, however, ended with a whimper as the women slowly began to disperse and head home. The shortages continued well into the postwar era of reconstruction, and the Bread Riot of 1863 quietly came to an end.

Mobile was known not only as a world-class port for exports at this time, but also for shipbuilding, and one famous craft that was built in the Port City was the first operational submarine, the CSS *Hunley*. The *Hunley* was built in the Park and Lyons Machine Shop on the corner of State and Water Streets in 1863. It had a long, narrow, almost tubular body that sat eight crew members. A long shaft with handles ran down the center of the submarine, with each of the sailors being positioned at each handle, cranking furiously to turn the ship's propeller as it glided silently just below the surface. Affixed to the bow of the ship was a long spar with a torpedo (mine) attached. The idea was for the *Hunley* to ram a ship with the spar, and the mine would explode, sinking the enemy ship.

The sub was transported by rail car to Charleston, South Carolina, with hopes that it would be able to clear the blockade that surrounded the city's harbor. During three separate practice runs, the sub sank; two of those sinkings saw the deaths of several crew members, prompting Confederate general Beauregard to comment that "it is more dangerous to those who use it than the enemy."

On February 17, 1864, the *Hunley* began its first—and last—historic mission. It set sail out of Charleston on a calm, moonlit night and headed toward its target, the USS *Housatonic*. The sailors aboard the Yankee ship began firing rifles at the sub, but the shells only pinged off its sides.

The spar and explosive plunged into the side of the *Housatonic* and detonated, ripping open a gaping hole. The ship sank in less than five minutes, killing 5 of its 155 member crew. The *Hunley*, however, never returned to port to celebrate its success. The sub sank forty-five minutes after the sinking of the *Housatonic*.

The final resting place of the *Hunley* and its crew was discovered in 1999, and in 2000, the sub was raised from its watery grave. Inside, what remained of the crew showed that they were still at their stations when the sub sank. It was determined that they died from pulmonary blast trauma.

The remains of the sailors were laid to rest in 2004 at White Points Garden Cemetery in Charleston. A memorial to the crew can be found in the Confederate section of Mobile's Magnolia Cemetery. A replica of the sub can be seen at the USS Alabama Battleship Park.

Back in 1864 Mobile, the citizens were finding ways around the blockade. In the first seven months of the year, shallow-draft vessels known as blockade runners made twenty-two attempts at slipping past the Union navy. Out of those, nineteen successfully sailed their cotton cargo out of the port and into the Gulf.

With the end of the war nowhere in sight, some of the troops stationed at Fort Morgan and around the city were becoming disillusioned with the war effort and attempted to rebel against the Confederacy. A reporter for the *Boston Journal* first reported that troops manning Fort Morgan at the mouth of Mobile Bay had taken control of the fort, saying that the "American flag was flying where the Rebel rag has so long floated."

A group of gunboats was dispatched from Mobile in an attempt to capture the garrison that had captured the fort but were turned away by gunfire. A larger force of men and ships headed to the fort and was able to recapture it. More than one hundred deserters were captured in the fort and at various locations surrounding Mobile. The report went on to say that seventy of the men were condemned to be shot the following morning.

The *Boston Journal* report also noted that morale among some of the Confederate troops in the city was waning:

> *The deserters bring the very important intelligence that the rebel army in and around Mobile have organized secret societies, and determined to fight no longer. It is said that the movement inaugurated among the soldiers is growing daily stronger and many officers are compromised in the movement.*

Throughout 1864, the fortunes of the Union were turning. Their troops were making significant inroads into the South with a string of major victories in the east that cut off Confederate general Robert E. Lee's supply lines, while General Sherman's men were barnstorming his troops through Georgia and South Carolina. It appeared that the war could end very soon. Only one Confederate port remained: Mobile. A *New York Times* reporter, Benjamin Clay, painted the picture:

> *Mobile, as I before informed you, is now next to Richmond the best fortified city in the Southern Confederacy. It has long been an eye sore to us, and some time ago—in fact immediately after the battle of Nashville—the great military eye of the republic was turned this way.*

As dawn broke on the morning of August 5, 1864, Union admiral David Farragut aboard the USS *Hartford* moved his fleet of eighteen warships—fourteen wooden vessels and four ironclads—into position near Fort Morgan to begin one of the most famous battles in U.S. naval history. The admiral gave the order, and the fleet began sailing north into Mobile Bay, his ironclads running parallel to the wooden ships on the starboard side to protect them from the expected cannon fire from the fort.

As Benjamin Clay had pointed out, Mobile was heavily fortified. Large wood pilings were driven into the shoals of the bay from Fort Gaines on Dauphin Island out into the mouth of the bay near the main shipping channel. Besides four hundred troops stationed at Fort Morgan, it also had twenty-four cannons. The Confederate navy's largest and most powerful ironclad, the CSS *Tennessee*, was stationed off the coast. The biggest defense against a Union invasion, however, were the mines (or, as they were called in the day, torpedoes), lacquer-coated wooden kegs and cone-shaped metal barrels packed with up to fifty pounds of black powder armed with primers that exploded when struck by a ship. The torpedoes were stretched in rows from east to west across the bay, narrowing the channel to only 500 feet wide and forcing any ships sailing in to maneuver within 150 feet of the fort's cannons.

The battle was on. One Confederate soldier described the sound of the cannons, saying, "The roar of cannon was like one continuous peal of thunder, deafening to the extreme."

Farragut climbed the rigging of the *Hartford* to watch his fleet's progress. As he watched, he saw the ironclad USS *Tecumseh* veer off course to pursue the *Tennessee*. As it crossed in front of the USS *Brooklyn*, the *Tecumseh* struck a mine and exploded. Quickly, the ship rolled over and sank to the shallow bottom of the bay, killing ninety-two crewmembers and its captain.

Seeing the disaster, Farragut allegedly gave an order that rallied his fleet and became famous worldwide: "Damn the torpedoes! Full speed ahead!" The fleet continued on and battled Confederate forces for three hours before a hole was blown in the side of the *Tennessee*. Soon after, Confederate admiral

DESTRUCTION OF THE MONITOR "TECUMSEH" BY A REBEL TORPEDO, IN MOBILE BAY, August 5, 1864.—[Sketched by Robert Weir.]

A line engraving after a sketch by Robert Weir, published in *Harper's Weekly*, September 10, 1864, depicting the loss of the USS *Tecumseh* during the Battle of Mobile Bay. *U.S. Naval History and Heritage Command.*

Franklin Buchannan ran up the white flag and surrendered the vessel. The Union navy had secured Mobile Bay. The city of Mobile was next.

Union soldiers landed on the eastern shore of Mobile Bay and headed north, while another garrison departed Pensacola, Florida, and headed west. Both divisions were heading for the town of Spanish Fort and the long since abandoned town of Blakeley that was now being used as Confederate outpost.

After slogging through swamps and heavy rain, 16,000 Federal troops descended on Fort Blakeley and faced off against 3,500 Confederates on August 9, 1865. When the Union troops arrived at the Confederate line, many Rebels turned and ran; others simply surrendered, while some stayed and fought in a fierce close-quarters battle.

In the end, 75 Confederate soldiers were killed, compared to 150 Union soldiers; two days later, only five miles west of Blakeley, Mobile mayor R.H. Sloane surrendered the city. The irony of the Battle of Blakeley was that as the troops faced off against each other, General Lee was surrendering to General Grant at Appomattox Courthouse, ending the Civil War. That fact made the Battle of Blakeley the last major battle of the Civil War.

Mobile was one of the lucky Southern cities. Federal troops peacefully crossed the bay and entered the city to take charge, but it wasn't completely safe. As the Union army moved in, arms and munitions that were surrendered were placed in storage in Marshall's Warehouse at the corner of Lipscomb and Commercial Streets, only feet from the Mobile River and bay.

One month after the surrender of the city, twenty tons of explosives stored in the building exploded. It was reported that eight city blocks were destroyed in the blast, which left an enormous crater where the building once stood. Fires continued the devastation, destroying the entire north section of the city and eight thousand bales of hay. In the river, the steamers *Cowles* and *Kate Dale* sank with all on board.

Federal troops immediately joined Mobilians to assist in putting out the fires and rescuing survivors. When the smoke had cleared, it was estimated that three hundred people were killed and scores wounded.

YOUR GUIDE TO HISTORY

Confederate Rest

5897 Pine Grove Drive, Fairhope
https://historichotels.org/us/hotels-resorts/grand-hotel-marriott-resort-golf-club-and-spa
Admission: Free

The eloquent Grand Hotel in Point Clear on the eastern shore of Mobile Bay was built in 1847. At that time, the hotel only had two floors and forty guest rooms. Guests had to arrive by ferryboat, which crossed the bay from Mobile. During the Civil War, as Admiral Farragut's Union navy made its way up the bay for the decisive battle that took the last Confederate port city, Mobile, the hotel was bombed. The hotel was converted into a field hospital, and between the Battle of Mobile Bay and the Battle of Blakeley, the hotel saw more than three thousand Confederate soldiers die within its walls. Many are buried at the Confederate Rest near the hotel, some buried shoulder-to-shoulder in mass graves. In 1869, a fire destroyed the records of the soldiers buried there, so bodies could not be identified. A large monument was erected to honor the unknown soldiers.

Fort Gaines

51 Bienville Road, Dauphin Island
(251) 861-6992
fort-gaines.com
Admission: Fee

Located directly across the mouth of Mobile Bay from Fort Morgan where the bay meets the Gulf of Mexico stands Fort Gaines, the Third System Fort that defended the western side of Mobile Bay. The fort saw action during the Battle of Mobile Bay in 1865. Today, living history reenactments and tours of the blacksmith shop, kitchen, cannons and myriad tunnels within the walls of the fort take place demonstrating what life was like not only at the fort but also on the island during the mid-1800s.

A view of one of the cannons ready for action at historic Fort Gaines. *Author's collection.*

The entrance through the massive stone portal of historic Fort Morgan. *Author's collection.*

Fort Morgan

110 Highway 180, Gulf Shores
(251) 540-5257
fort-morgan.org
Admission: Fee

Only twenty-two miles west of the glorious seaside town of Gulf Shores is historic Fort Morgan, site of the Battle of Mobile Bay. Spend a day exploring the many rooms and tunnels of the fort, as well as batteries built to guard the coastline during World War II. The fort has a fascinating museum and well-stocked gift shop. The best time to visit is the first weekend of August, when the Battle of Mobile Bay is reenacted. Visit its website for dates and times and plan to arrive early. It is a major draw for visitors to Alabama's pristine white Gulf beaches.

Historic Blakely State Park

34745 AL 225, Spanish Fort
(251) 626-0798
blakeleypark.com
Admission: Fee

The site of the last major battle of the Civil War holds more history than for just that eventful day in 1865. Within its two thousand acres, you can explore Native American history; the remains of the town of Blakeley, which once rivaled Mobile as the region's most successful port city; and, of course, the battlefield, with some of the best-preserved redoubts and earthen breastworks in the region. Make plans to visit the beginning of April (dates and times are available on the website) for the Battle of Blakeley living history and reenactment weekend.

Magnolia Cemetery

1202 Virginia Street, Mobile
(251) 432-8672
magnoliacemetery.com
Admission: Free

Only blocks from downtown Mobile, Magnolia Cemetery was established in 1836 in what was then outside the city limits, replacing the old Church

Historic Blakeley State Park has some of the best-preserved Civil War breastworks and earthworks in the South. *Author's collection.*

An example of the beautiful Victorian-era funerary works at Magnolia Cemetery. *Author's collection.*

Street Cemetery. At the time, the cemetery was only 36 acres, but today it encompasses 120 acres and is the final resting place of many of Mobile's most famous people: the founder of Mardi Gras and the Cowbellion de Rakin Society's Michael Krafft; Dr. Josiah C. Nott, the physician who first reported that mosquitoes transmitted yellow fever; and many more. The cemetery is also the resting place of many Confederate soldiers from the area who fought in the Civil War and includes a special memorial to the crew of the first operational submarine, the CSS *Hunley*, which was built in Mobile.

USS *Tecumseh*
110 Highway 180, Gulf Shores
(251) 540-5257
fort-morgan.org
Admission: Fee

When visiting Fort Morgan, pay a visit to the north side of the fort and walk down the old fishing ramp to the shores of Mobile Bay. There in the lapping waves is a buoy marking the military grave site of the USS *Tecumseh*, which sank after hitting a torpedo mine during the Battle of Mobile Bay. Ninety-two sailors perished aboard the ship. Visit during the annual reenactment of the battle the first week of August each year and take part in the moving service held to honor those who were lost.

Chapter 10

ALABAMA'S PORT CITY

s we have seen, life around Mobile was all about the water—the rivers, the delta, the bay and the Gulf of Mexico. The city's golden age occurred when cotton was king during the antebellum period, but over the centuries, Mobile has learned to adapt its waterfront to a variety of changes and challenges.

Long before Interstate 10 and the Mobile Bay Causeway (U.S. Highway 90/98) were built, the prime method for crossing the bay was by ferryboats. Flat-bottom and later paddle-wheel boats like the *Alvares* and *Cleveland* regularly sailed cross the bay from downtown Mobile to the pier at Fairhope on the bay's eastern shore with full loads of passengers.

Shipping has always been an essential part of the Mobile economy. When British rule over the city began following the French and Indian War in 1863, the port began to boom with an unusual cargo: deer hides.

While there were only three hundred or so settlers in the city at the time, the area was filled with Native Americans, thousands of them from the Cherokee, Choctaw, Creek and many other different tribes. By this time, the indigenous people had acquired quite an arsenal of weapons from the Europeans who had settled the area, and with those, they would hold mass hunting of white-tailed deer. The pelts were sold to the colonists, who would then ship them to England and other ports to be made into hats, coats, handbags and more.

The early twentieth century saw Mobile's docks transform once again, this time to accommodate the growing desire of the nation for something we take for granted today: bananas. Beginning in the 1880s, American businessman Andrew Preston sampled an exotic fruit in the Caribbean and made a bet that Americans would clamor over it in the states. That exotic fruit was a variety of bananas called Gros Michel. Preston and his associate, Minor Cooper Keith, purchased large tracts of land in Jamaica, cleared the land and began growing the fruit with the hopes that Americans would take to the yellow-skinned fruit.

The businessmen set up their own steamship company and began exporting the fruit to Boston and New York, where they had built a network of ice-cooled warehouses to store the fruit. With a bombardment of advertising, the businessmen correctly predicted that bananas would be more popular than apples in the United States, and it was off to the races as other countries joined in to bring the fruit to U.S. markets, including the "banana republics" of Costa Rica, Honduras and Guatemala.

In Mobile, the warehouses along the waterfront were transformed with those ice-cooled warehouses being added, and soon, the downtown waterfront became known as the "Banana Docks." By 1937, Mobile was the third-largest importer of the fruit in the United States.

Mobile's harbor also focused on shipbuilding. In the earliest days of the city, under French rule, the tall, longleaf pines that grew around the bay were perfect for shipbuilding. With the outbreak of World War I, one would think that Mobile would be in perfect position to fill the need for ships, but in fact, with inadequate facilities to handle large merchant ships and a lack of trained labor, only one ship built in Mobile was launched before the end of the war.

The "Mighty A," the USS *Alabama*, is moored dockside on Mobile Bay, inviting visitors to explore its storied history, vintage airplanes and the World War II submarine USS *Drum*. *Author's collection.*

Enter John B. Waterman. Waterman moved to Mobile from New Orleans in 1902 to work for the railroads. With the aid of Mobile Coca-Cola bottler Walter Bellingrath, lumber executive C.W. Hempstead and Mobile mayor T.M. Stevens, the group formed the Waterman Steamship Company. With $2,000 and a ship on loan from the U.S. Shipping Board, the company began shipping construction materials, including lumber, to Florida, eventually expanding their business, building more and more ships and shipping goods to the islands in the Caribbean.

When the Great Depression hit the nation, one saving grace for Mobile was the Waterman Steamship Company, which greatly expanded its labor force and soon operated 125 vessels worldwide, manned by nine hundred merchant marines. Following World War II, Waterman was the largest shipping company in the world.

In the late 1930s, as the clouds of war broke out into a storm in Europe, Mobile shipbuilders were contracted by the federal government to build Liberty ships and destroyers. By the time the United States had entered World War II, the city's shipbuilding industry was booming. The Waterman Company switched gears for the war effort and had the largest merchant fleets plying the seas. Gulf Shipbuilding started 1940 off with only 240 employees. By 1941, it had more than 11,000, while the Alabama Dry Dock went from 1,000 workers to 30,000.

By 1944, the city's population had swelled 64 percent up to almost 300,000. The city became so overcrowded that people flocking to the city for jobs were sleeping in vacant lots. Boardinghouses would rent rooms to four people at a time.

Even African Americans flocked into the Port City looking for work, as the government required that all defense contractors would "engage in non-discriminatory practices," and more than 2,500 women started work at Alabama Dry Dock.

One naval vessel that wasn't built in Mobile but still holds a special place in the hearts of Mobilians is the "Mighty A," the USS *Alabama*. Berthed at the USS Alabama Battleship Memorial Park, the *Alabama* began its storied career during World War II in 1943 in the Atlantic, culminating in leading the American fleet into Tokyo Bay on September 5, 1945, at the end of the war after earning nine battle stars.

In 1962, the *Alabama* was destined for the scrap pile, but thousands of Mobilians rallied around it and brought the battleship to Mobile Bay, where it is now the centerpiece of the park. Also at the park, visitors can view World War II aircraft and the submarine USS *Drum* and pay tribute to those

Workers transfer bananas from a freighter to a waiting railroad car at Mobile's old Banana docks in 1937. *U.S. Resettlement Administration, Arthur Rothstein, photographer,* Loading Bananas, *Mobile, Alabama, 1937.*

Whether it's coal, steel, shipping containers or building or refitting U.S. Navy vessels, Mobile Harbor is still the main player in the city's economy after more than three hundred years. *Author's collection.*

who have fought for the country at the many moving monuments to these men and women.

Today, the Port of Mobile is as busy as ever. The Australian company Austal is currently under contract to build new Littoral Combat Ships (LCS) and Expeditionary Fast Transport (EFT) ships for the U.S. Navy. The dry docks are regularly filled with navy and commercial ships in for repair, and the shipping container business is the busiest it has ever been. In fact, after the supply shortage during the COVID-19 outbreak, the container port has seen an increase in shipments of 80 percent.

The newest addition to Mobile's harbor is the state-of-the-art cruise terminal, where residents of the city and travelers from across the country can set sail on the Carnival cruise ship the *Spirit* to the western Caribbean and Bahamas.

It's only fitting that on the banks of the river and bay that brought Mobile to life stands a museum dedicated to the city's maritime history and that of the Gulf Coast: the GulfQuest National Maritime Museum of the Gulf of Mexico.

YOUR GUIDE TO HISTORY

GulfQuest National Maritime Museum of the Gulf of Mexico

155 South Water Street, Mobile
(251) 436-8901
gulfquest.org
Admission: Fee

Explore the maritime history of Mobile and the Gulf of Mexico in this unique museum located on Mobile's waterfront. There are plenty of interactive exhibits for young and old to explore.

Located on Mobile's riverfront at Cooper Riverside Park, the GulfQuest museum tells the history of maritime Mobile as well as the entire Gulf Coast with interactive displays and presentations. *Author's collection.*

Harbor Tours/Middle Bay Lighthouse Tour

30945 Five Rivers Boulevard, Spanish Fort
(251) 626-0798
blakeleypark.com/Cruises
Admission: Fee

Hop aboard the *Delta Explorer* for an up-close tour of Mobile harbor. See ships being built and the massive shipping container port and learn even more of the city's maritime history. The *Delta Explorer* also has tours to the Middle Bay Lighthouse. Patterned after the famous lighthouses of Chesapeake Bay, Middle Bay is a hexagonal lighthouse that was built in 1885.

Mobile Bay Ferry

112 Bienville Boulevard, Dauphin Island, with opposite boarding at Historic Fort Morgan, 110 AL 180, Gulf Shores
(251) 861-3000
mobilebayferry.com
Admission: Fee (either walk on or drive on)

Take an enjoyable forty-five-minute ride across the mouth of Mobile Bay between Dauphin Island and historic Fort Gaines on the Mobile Bay Ferry. Passengers can either walk on or take the car. Either way, it is a fun ride, and maybe you will catch some dolphins en route.

The *Rachel*

Beach Boulevard (AL Highway 182), Gulf Shores, fifteen miles west of the intersection of U.S. Highway 59 and AL Highway 180; GPS coordinates: N 30°13'53.5", W 87°55'51.2"W
Admission: Free

During the height of Mobile's lumber boom in 1923, the wooden schooner *Rachel* faced a massive tropical storm as it attempted to head into Mobile Bay and was facing imminent danger—raging seas, blinding rain and howling winds. Despite having dropped its anchor, the *Rachel* drifted toward shore along the Fort Morgan Peninsula at the mouth of the bay, dragging its anchor. The ship ran aground. The crew stayed on board and survived the storm, and as for the *Rachel*, it's still stuck in the sand west of Gulf Shores. You can see the remains of the *Rachel*, or rather what's left of the ship, its ribs and keel, on the beach. But here's the rub—you can only see it sometimes. The action of the Gulf currents continually bury the *Rachel* in fine sand, and when the next hurricane or strong tropical storm blows through, it is uncovered again. Please be courteous to the homeowners who have houses in the area and please don't block Beach Boulevard.

USS *Alabama* Battleship Memorial Park
2703 Battleship Parkway (U.S. Highway 90/U.S. Highway 98), Mobile
(251) 432-0261
ussalabama.com
Admission: Fee

Explore the enormous USS *Alabama* battleship. You can visit not only the battleship but also acres of aircraft from different eras, including World War II; you can also explore an actual World War II submarine, the USS *Drum*, and pay tribute to those who gave their all for the country at the park's moving memorials.

Chapter 11

IT MUST BE THE WATER

BASEBALL IN MOBILE

Next to Mardi Gras, the one thing that Mobilians are most proud of is the city's role in baseball history. Not only is Mobile the birthplace of five Major League Baseball Hall of Fame players, the third-highest number of players born in a single city after New York and Los Angeles, but it has also played home to a dizzying number of other players who either hail from the Port City or have honed their skills there in one of the many minor-league teams that have been fielded over the years.

In the words of one of the city's most famous players, Henry "Hank" Aaron when asked why that was, he replied, "It must be the water."

While there is no official date as to when the game was first played in the city, we do know that it was played as far back as the 1860s, just prior to the Civil War. Along Spring Hill Avenue, the state's oldest institution of higher learning, Spring Hill College was playing the game on its campus.

While researching our book *Baseball in Mobile* (Arcadia Publishing) back in 2004, coauthor Tamra Carraway and I first introduced the world to a little-known fact (at the time) that the baseball craze on the island of Cuba began in Mobile at Spring Hill, when two brothers from the island, Nemesio and Earnest Guillo, enrolled in the college. During their stay, they fell in love with the sport, so much so that when the Civil War ended and the blockade of Mobile Bay was lifted, the brothers returned to their homeland with more than a degree. They also brought with them the first baseballs and bats. Nemesio went on to form the first professional team on the island in 1878, Club Havana, as well as the first league, the Cuban Professional League.

Long before the advent of the Negro League, Black ball players were taking to the field in Mobile as early as the late 1880s. Short one- or two-line mentions hidden in the pages of the *Mobile Register* or *New Orleans Times-Democrat* were the only indications that there were Black teams. For example, in the September 25, 1894 edition of the *Times-Picayune*, the paper noted, "The Mobile colored baseball team cleaned up the Pensacola colored club at Frascati Park last evening to the tune of 11 to 6." And that was it. Nothing else about the players or play was mentioned.

As the rules of the game became formalized, more and more professional teams began springing up around the country, including in Mobile. In 1886, the Port City fielded two pro teams—Club Mobile and the Acid Iron Earth Baseball Club. The latter was named after their sponsor—a locally produced miracle elixir that contained "nothing but what is contained in the Earth." Both early teams played in a four team league called the Gulf Baseball League. The other two teams were both from New Orleans—the Robert E. Lees and the Club New Orleans. The Acid Iron team was the first U.S. baseball team to travel to a foreign country to play a game, completing the Mobile-to-Cuba baseball circle when they played a game in Havana.

Mobile's first pro team, Acid Iron Earth, pictured in 1886. Managed by "Honest" John Kelly, the team was the first American team to travel to a foreign country (Cuba) to play a game. *Author's collection.*

These early teams—both Black and white—in Mobile first played at Frascati Park, the largest and most popular city park in Port City. Frascati was located two miles south of downtown Mobile in an area known as Choctaw Point, where one of the city's founders, Bienville, had built a "mansion" just after the city's founding called Chateaux Bienville.

Frascati Park was located directly on Mobile Bay, where cool bay breezes continually blew in from the east, the gnarled limbs of live oaks gracefully adorned with flowing Spanish moss provided much-needed shade in the heat of summer and the fragrant perfume of those flowering magnolias filled the air. The park was the hub of activity for Mobilians, with several baseball fields, an open-air pavilion, concession stands and a long pier that stretched out into the bay.

The first official minor-league team from Mobile to play at Frascati, the Mobile Oyster Grabbers, joined the Southern Interstate League in 1903. After only one season, the team folded but was soon replaced in 1905 when the Natchez (Mississippi) Indians of the Class "D" Cotton States League hightailed it out of town due to a yellow fever epidemic and made their home in Mobile as the Mobile Sea Gull–Oystermen. That same yellow fever epidemic swept across the South, and the 1905 season was canceled only one month after the opening pitch, but it would return the following year and see the Gulls win back-to-back championships in 1906 and 1907.

The Sea Gull–Oystermen was a team to be reckoned with, but they had an identity crisis, changing names multiple times over the ensuing years: Mobile Sea Gull–Fishermen, Mobile Reed Birds and Mobile Sea Gulls. They finally settled on the name the Mobile Bears. Manager Pat Flaherty told the press that a bear is tough: "He can bite. He can claw. He can hug. He can fight at the drop of a hat. Sea Gulls don't mean a thing in the world."

The Bears played in the minor-league Southern Association, the forerunner of today's AAA Southern League, playing to huge crowds at Monroe Park, a new park also located on the banks of Mobile Bay on the old Bay Shell Road. The park was described as the "Coney Island of the South," with an eclectic array of amusement rides, concerts, dancing, swimming in the bay and, of course, baseball, with 6,500 fans cheering on the Bears from the bleachers.

Baseball had become a city passion. By 1918, the stands were routinely sold out, and on opening day of that year, the entire city literally shut down to watch as the Bears defeated the team from New Orleans by a score of 9–0. The sport became so popular in Mobile that the city petitioned the Alabama state legislature to allow the Bears to play games on Sunday, which, at the

The carousel, the centerpiece of Mobile's Monroe Park, the "Coney Island of the South." *Detroit Publishing Company,* The Carousel, *Monroe Park, Mobile, Alabama, [between 1900 and 1915], https://www.loc.gov/item/2016811106.*

time, was against state law. The petition made it through the statehouse, and baseball was made a seven-day-a-week sport in the state.

Major League Baseball took notice, and teams from the big cities across the country came to Mobile to play exhibition and spring training games, including the 1909 World Champion Chicago Cubs, who played a five-game exhibition series against the Spring Hill Badgers college team. Joe Tinker of "Tinker to Evers to Chance" double-play fame umpired the games. And it was no surprise to see the likes of New York Yankee great Babe Ruth appear at a Spring Hill game, where he would give home run demonstrations to wild fans.

This was the beginning of Mobile's baseball golden years. In 1927, a new stadium was built, Hartwell Field, on the corner of Tennessee and Ann Streets, and a parade of future major-league standouts would hone their craft on its field—future TV series *The Rifleman* star Chuck Connors, Boston Red Sox great and future manager Don Zimmer, Dodgers outfielder George "Shotgun" Shuba and Mobile's own Frank and Milt Bolling.

The Great Bambino, Babe Ruth, swaps his bat for a tuba during an exhibition visit to Mobile's Spring Hill College in 1924. *Dr. Charles Boyle, Spring Hill College.*

But by 1961, the frenzy had died out. The Mobile Bears shut down that year, and Hartwell Field fell silent, eventually being demolished. For the next thirty-six years until the establishment of the Mobile Bay Bears and the construction of Hank Aaron Stadium in 1996, Mobile was virtually devoid of any major- or minor-league baseball save for a few meager attempts at resurrecting it with the short-lived Mobile Bay Sharks in the '90s and a flirtation with being the home of the Birmingham Barons minor-league team in the mid-1960s when their owner, Charlie Finley, had a dispute with vendors at his stadium in Birmingham, Alabama, and moved the team to Mobile for one season. During that year, future greats from the Oakland A's dynasty teams roamed Hartwell Field, including Sal Bando, Tony LaRussa, Rick Monday and more.

As you can see, Mobile has had a storied baseball history, but what makes the story of baseball in Mobile amazing is that behind this minor-league façade, some of the game's greatest players were making a name for themselves, struggling through incredible racial barriers to reach the pinnacle of the game, and were homegrown heroes from Mobile and its suburbs. The first was a young teenager named Leroy Paige.

These boys catch a game from outside the outfield fence at Hartwell Field. *City of Mobile Archives.*

At an early age, Paige took a job at a local railway station in his hometown as a porter, where he would carry passengers' luggage for ten cents per bag. The tall, lanky teen perfected carrying several suitcases at a time and was called a "walking satchel tree" by his coworkers. The nickname "Satchel" stuck.

Satchel Paige would spend hours at his home practicing throwing baseballs at moveable targets, mostly birds, who never saw the ball coming. Baseball wasn't a dream of his per se. It was a diversion from the racial segregation of the day—that is, until a former acquaintance and player-manager for the Negro League's Chattanooga Black Lookouts paid Satchel a visit and signed him to a contract to play with the team for fifty dollars a month (most of which was sent back home to his mother).

Paige's career took off, seeing him playing for different teams in the Negro League and with some of the best Black players in the game, many of whom also came from Mobile themselves: "the fastest man in baseball" James Thomas "Cool Papa" Bell, Ted "Double Duty" Radcliffe, "the human vacuum" Bobby Robinson and one Henry "Hank" Aaron.

Satchel made quite a name for himself with his perfect pitching arm and cocky bravado. As a reporter following the Negro League once said, "Negro baseball had in Satchel Paige the rare asset that Babe Ruth had been for the white major leagues—a humorous, colorful, engaging bragger with a child-like personality, who just happened to be able to justify his boasts on the playing field. When had any pitcher been so outrageously arrogant and taunting as to send the infield to the dugout while he faced the best hitters in the opposition lineup?"

At the age of forty-two, Paige became the oldest rookie in Major League Baseball, signing on with the Cleveland Indians, with whom he won twenty-eight games over six years. He was elected to the Baseball Hall of Fame in 1971 and passed away just eleven years later on June 8, 1982.

"Sweet Swingin'" Billy Williams was born in 1938 in what was, at the time, an unincorporated area of Mobile County that is now part of Prichard, a suburb of Mobile. Williams's career began in 1955, playing for the Mobile Black Bears and the Chicago Cubs' farm team in the Class "D" Sooner State League. He nearly left the game altogether in 1959 when he encountered overt racism while playing in Texas on a Double "A" Texas League team.

Disillusioned by the experience, Williams returned to Mobile, where it looked like his career would end, but within a week, a scout for the Cubs, Buck O'Neil, convinced him to return to the game, which he did. Williams eventually made his major-league debut at Wrigley Field on August 6, 1959. By the end of his career, Williams had 2,711 hits and 426 home runs and at one time held the National League record for playing in the most consecutive games at 1,117. Williams was elected to the Hall of Fame in 1987.

One Hall of Famer whom most people don't know is originally from Mobile is the "Wizard of Oz," Ozzie Smith. Smith wasn't known for his batting, but his spectacular acrobatic defensive play on the field made him recognized as one of the "greatest defensive shortstops of all time." As pitcher Gaylord Perry once said, "I was always hoping they would hit the ball his way because I knew then that my trouble was over." Smith's thirteen Golden Gloves opened the door for his induction to the Hall of Fame in 2002.

Another Mobile Hall of Famer was one of baseball's premier power hitters, Willie McCovey. McCovey was born in Mobile on January 10, 1938. The seventh of ten children, the young Willie took on several jobs to help support his family—newspaper boy, clearing tables at a whites-only restaurant and working in a bakery. He was deeply affected by the racial injustices his family endured while growing up, including hearing his father being addressed as "boy."

His love of baseball began by listening to games on the radio and then playing the sport on local playgrounds. A former Negro League team owner, Alex Pompez, saw McCovey play and brought him to the attention of the New York Giants, for whom he played for most of his career, becoming a legend when the team moved to San Francisco. By the end of his career, McCovey had 1,555 runs batted in and was so feared by pitchers that he was intentionally walked innumerable times. In 1969, he set the (at the time) record for being intentionally walked at forty-five times. Former Cincinnati Reds manager Sparky Anderson called him the "most feared man in baseball." McCovey was elected to the Hall of Fame in 1986.

The fifth and final name in the list of Mobile baseball Hall of Famers is a name that, when it comes to baseball, is the most recognizable in the city. It's unavoidable, being seen on parks, streets and stadiums. In the summer of 1952, a scout for the Negro League's Indianapolis Clowns, Ed Scott, went out to a local ball field in a Mobile suburb to watch a fast-pitch softball game and saw a young man hitting "the ball like crazy," but he did it with a unique grip on the bat—crisscrossed hands. It was seventeen-year-old Henry Aaron.

Scott went to Aaron's parents to ask if Henry could sign on with the team. His mother refused to let her boy go. It was Aaron's father who finally gave permission, and soon, Hank was standing at a Mobile train station with a bag in his hand that held two sandwiches and two pairs of pants and two dollars in his pocket to begin an incredible career.

It was indeed the beginning of a legend. Not only did Aaron break the unbreakable record held by Babe Ruth by hitting 715 home runs in 1974, but he also set other records, including the all-time RBI record of 2,297. During his ride to the home run record, Aaron faced incredible racial hatred, including death threats, but through it all, he stayed steady and consistent, taking the advice his mother, Estelle, had given him to heart: "Don't worry about that which you have no control over."

The pressure Aaron felt as he neared the home run record was incredible, and he compared his situation with Roger Maris when the Yankee great hit sixty-four home runs in one year. "Roger Maris lost his hair the season he hit 64," Aaron told a reporter in an interview. "I still have my hair, but when this is over, I'm going home to Mobile to fish for a long time."

In the end, "Hammerin'" Hank Aaron hit 755 homeruns, 3,016 hits and an all-time RBI record of 2,297. He was inducted into the Hall of Fame in 1982.

Besides the five Hall of Fame players from Mobile, the city is the birthplace of many other baseball notables, including Cleon Jones, Tommy Agee and Amos Otis, all of whom played on the "Amazing" Mets of 1969. The team went from loveable losers who couldn't win a game to save their lives during their inaugural season in 1962 to winning the World Series in only seven years, becoming the "Miracle Mets" in 1969. The team fielded an incredible lineup of players and pitchers, including Tom Seaver, Jerry Koosman and those "Mets from Mobile." The thrilling diving catches of Agee and the emotional final out made by Jones in the final game of the Series cemented their names in baseball history.

There was a resurgence of baseball in Mobile in 1997 when the new Hank Aaron Stadium opened its doors and a brand new minor-league team, the Mobile Bay Bears, took to the field. Taking in a game at the stadium was highlighted with a chance to visit Aaron's childhood home, which was moved to the ballpark on Bolling Brothers Boulevard and opened as a museum.

It is a sad ending to this chapter of Mobile history to say that in 2019, twenty-two years after the Bay Bears came to Mobile, the team folded. Baseball in Mobile came to an end, but knowing the city, a new team will eventually take the Bay Bears' place and the tradition of baseball in the Port City will continue.

YOUR GUIDE TO HISTORY

Hall of Fame Courtyard at Cooper Riverside Park

101 South Water Street, Mobile
(251) 208-5311
Admission: Free

Currently under construction as of this writing, Mobile's waterfront at Cooper Riverside Park will have a special place set aside for its five Hall of Fame players and other notables from the city who made it to the big leagues. It will be called the Hall of Fame Courtyard and will be anchored by five nine-foot-tall, six-hundred- to nine-hundred-pound bronze sculptures of the city's famous Hall of Famers created by Grand Rapids, Michigan artist Brett Grill. The completed courtyard will feature an empty pedestal where you can take a selfie with the hometown heroes. More interactive displays will be announced after the initial courtyard is completed.

Hank Aaron Park

Corner of Andrews and Helveston Streets, Mobile (Toulminville community)
Admission: Free

Located only two blocks from where Hank Aaron's childhood home once stood, the Henry "Hank" Aaron Park (formerly Carver Park) was renamed in honor of the slugger in 1991 and now has baseball-themed playgrounds and, of course, baseball diamonds for residents young and old to enjoy. At its heart, the park has a large stone statue in the shape of Alabama, with an image of Aaron hitting his 715th home run etched into it. The statue is surrounded by the names of the other Mobile Hall of Famers.

Hank Aaron's Childhood Home

755 Bolling Brothers Boulevard, Mobile
(251) 572-2327
mobile.org/listing/hank-aaron-childhood-home-%26-museum/600
Admission: Free

Step inside the original home of Henry "Hank" Aaron. The home was moved to its currently location next to Hank Aaron Stadium and is now a museum filled with memorabilia from Aaron's childhood and baseball career. As of this writing, the museum and Hank Aaron Stadium are only open for special events. Check the website for details. Discussion is underway to move the home once again to a new location for the public to enjoy.

Springhill College Stan Galle Field (aka "The Pit")

Avenue of the Oaks, Mobile
(800) 742-6704
shcbadgers.com/facilities/historic-stan-galle-field/2
Admission: Free during off season; fee during the baseball season (visit the website)

Since 1889, Stan Galle Field (named after one of Spring Hill College's former baseball coaches) has been fielding intercollegiate ball games. In fact, it is believed to be the oldest active college ball field in the country. Not much has changed from when the field opened to present day.

University of South Alabama/Stanky Field

Half a mile west of the intersection of Old Shell Road and University Boulevard, Mobile
University of South Alabama Baseball Office, Mitchell Center,
Room 1209, Mobile
(251) 461-1872
usajaguars.com/sports/baseball
Admission: Fee for games

Next to the many minor-league baseball teams Mobile has fielded, the University of South Alabama Jaguars have produced many major-leaguers: Mike O'Berry, Dave Stapleton, Lance Johnson and Luis Gonzalez, to name only a few. The Jags have consistently led college baseball's Sun Belt Conference, and every game is pure excitement to watch.

SELECTED BIBLIOGRAPHY

WEBSITES

Each site that I have taken you to in this book has one or more incredibly valuable websites that dig deeper into the history described. I encourage you to visit them to learn more and to check their latest hours of operation and admission fees (if applicable). Be sure to check their event calendars as well. You never know what you will find and where your next journey will lead to. Here are a few other websites of interest for additional Mobile and Alabama Gulf Coast history.

Alabama Heritage Magazine. alabamaheritage.com. This is a reliable website for articles by both Alabama historians and archaeologists.

Encyclopedia of Alabama. encylopediaofalabama.org.

Mobile Bay Magazine. mobilebaymag.com. You will find many articles by Mobile historian John Sledge here.

Mobile Mask. mobilemask.com. This is this definitive site on Mardi Gras in Mobile.

BOOKS

Amos, Harriet E. *Cotton City: Urban Development in Antebellum Mobile*. Tuscaloosa: University of Alabama Press, 1985.

Brueske, Paul. *The Last Siege*. Havertown, PA: Casemate Publishers, 2018.

Brunson, James E., III. *Black Baseball: 1858–1900*. Jefferson, NC: McFarland & Company, 2019.

Bunn, Mike. *Fourteenth Colony: The Forgotten Story of the Gulf South during America's Revolutionary Era*. Montgomery, AL: New South Books, 2020.

Cuhaj, Joe. *Hidden History of Mobile*. Charleston, SC: The History Press. 2019.

Cuhaj, Joe, and Tamra Carraway-Hinckle. *Baseball in Mobile*. Charleston, SC: Arcadia Publishing, 2004.

Hamilton, Peter Joseph. *Colonial Mobile*. Boston: Houghton, Mifflin and Company, 1898.

Higgenbotham, Jay. *Mobile: City by the Bay*. Mobile, AL: Azalea City Printers, 1968.

———. *Old Mobile: Fort Louis de la Louisiane, 1702–1711*. Tuscaloosa: University of Alabama Press, 1977.

Hurston, Zora Neale. *Barracoon: The Story of the Last "Black Cargo."* New York: Amistad Press, 2018.

Kirby, Brendan. *Wicked Mobile*. Charleston, SC: The History Press, 2015.

Morton, Patricia. *Discovering the Women in Slavery*. Athens: University of Georgia Press, 1996.

Raines, Ben. *The Last Slave Ship*. New York: Simon & Schuster, 2022.

Roberts, L. Greg. *Mardi Gras in Mobile*. Charleston, SC: The History Press, 2015.

Schell, Sidney Henson. *The Continental Navy on the Gulf Coast, 1775–1781: The USS West Florida at the Siege of Mobile 1780*. Mobile, AL: Sidney H. Schell, 2014.

Shorter, George W. *The Late Woodland Period of the Lower Tombigbee River*. Mobile: Center for Archaeological Studies at the University of South Alabama, 1999.

Sledge, John. *The Last Slave Ship*. New York: Simon & Schuster, 2022.

———. *The Mobile River*. Columbia: University of South Carolina Press, 2015.

Smithweck, David. *The USS* Tecumseh *in Mobile Bay*. Charleston, SC: The History Press, 2021.

Thompson, Alan Smith. *Mobile, Alabama, 1850–1861: Economic, Political, Physical, and Population Characteristics*. Tuscaloosa: University of Alabama Press, 1979.

Thornton, J. Mills, III. *Politics and Power in a Slave Society: Alabama, 1800–1860*. Baton Rouge: Louisiana State University Press, 1978.

Webb, Paula Lenor. *Such a Woman: The Life of Madame Octavia Walton LeVert*. Bristol, UK: Intellect Books, 2021.

ABOUT THE AUTHOR

Former radio broadcaster turned software programmer turned author Joe Cuhaj moved to the Alabama Gulf Coast more than forty years ago and immediately fell in love with the area's rich history. In 2004, along with coauthor Tamra Carraway, Cuhaj wrote his first book on Mobile history, *Baseball in Mobile* (Arcadia Publishing). His second book, *Hidden History of Mobile* (The History Press, 2020), brought some of the unknown and forgotten stories of the Port City's past to life. In addition to his Mobile history books, Cuhaj is also the author of nine outdoor recreational guides to the state on hiking, paddling and camping for Falcon Books. He has also authored two new historical books related to the space program: *Space Oddities: Forgotten Stories of Mankind's Exploration of Space* (Prometheus Books, 2022) and *Everyone's Gone to the Moon* (Prometheus Books, 2023). You can learn more about Joe's books, download his podcasts and read his short stories on his website (joe-cuhaj.com).